PROTECT YOUR WEALTH FROM THE RAVAGES OF INFLATION

Paul M. King

Apress®

Protect Your Wealth from the Ravages of Inflation

ISBN-13 (pbk): 978-1-4302-3822-5

ISBN-13 (electronic): 978-1-4302-3823-2

Trademarked names, logos, and images may appear in this book. Rather than use a trademark symbol with every occurrence of a trademarked name, logo, or image we use the names, logos, and images only in an editorial fashion and to the benefit of the trademark owner, with no intention of infringement of the trademark.

The use in this publication of trade names, trademarks, service marks, and similar terms, even if they are not identified as such, is not to be taken as an expression of opinion as to whether or not they are subject to proprietary rights.

President and Publisher: Paul Manning
Lead Editor: Jeff Olson
Editorial Board: Steve Anglin, Mark Beckner, Ewan Buckingham, Gary Cornell, Jonathan Gennick, Jonathan Hassell, Michelle Lowman, Matthew Moodie, Jeff Olson, Jeffrey Pepper, Frank Pohlmann, Douglas Pundick, Ben Renow-Clarke, Dominic Shakeshaft, Matt Wade, Tom Welsh
Coordinating Editor: Adam Heath
Copy Editor: Damon Larson
Compositor: Mary Sudul
Indexer: SPi Global
Artist: SPi Global
Cover Designer: Anna Ishchenko

Distributed to the book trade worldwide by Springer Science+Business Media, LLC., 233 Spring Street, 6th Floor, New York, NY 10013. Phone 1-800-SPRINGER, fax (201) 348-4505, e-mail orders-ny@springer-sbm.com, or visit www.springeronline.com.

For information on translations, please e-mail rights@apress.com, or visit www.apress.com.

Apress and friends of ED books may be purchased in bulk for academic, corporate, or promotional use. eBook versions and licenses are also available for most titles. For more information, reference our Special Bulk Sales–eBook Licensing web page at www.apress.com/info/bulksales.

For my son, Josh,
the inspiration for everything I do

Contents

About the Author

Paul M. King is owner, head trader, trading coach, and financial consultant at PMKing Trading, LLC. His background is in information systems, but he moved from technology to the business side as a consultant to Wall Street companies. King is passionate about trading and helping traders improve their performance through his international mentoring program. He has trading clients all over the world, including in the United States, Canada, South America, and Australia. As well as sharing his insights on his blog, mini-eBooks about trading, and articles published in *Futures* magazine and elsewhere, King is very interested in personal finance and helping his clients become wealthier. Author of *The Complete Guide to Building a Successful Trading Business*, King's philosophy on trading and life in general is summed up by this old Chinese proverb: "Those who say a thing is impossible should not interrupt the people doing it."

Acknowledgments

First, I'd like to thank the governments of the world and their wonderful fiat currencies and interesting monetary and fiscal policies—without which this book would not be useful or required.

On a less facetious note, I'd also sincerely like to thank Jeff Olson, the lead editor of this book, without whom I would never, ever, have gotten around to doing a brain dump of all the information I've accumulated by helping various financial advice clients over the years. Jeff, many thanks for your initial gentle prodding to consider writing this book in the first place, your tireless editorial improvements, and your unique ability to let me know when I was assuming my readers would know what the heck I was talking about when it was obvious to you they wouldn't (because you didn't). This book is much, much better than it would have been if I'd ever bothered to self-publish it (which is doubtful). Thank you.

Acronyms, Abbreviations, and Symbols

ADV	Average daily volume
AMEX	American Stock Exchange
ATR	Average true range
AUD	Australian dollar
CAD	Canadian dollar
CAGR	Compound annual growth rate
CD	Certificate of deposit
CHF	Swiss franc
CPI	Consumer Price Index
CPI-U	Consumer Price Index for All Urban Consumers
DD	Drawdown
EEM	iShares MSCI Emerging Markets Index Fund ETF
EFA	iShares Trust MSCI EAFE Index
EPI	WisdomTree India Earnings ETF

ETF	Exchange-traded fund
EUM	ProShares Short MSCI Emerging Markets ETF
EUR	Euro
EWA	iShares MSCI Australia Index ETF
EWC	iShares MSCI Canada Index ETF
EWG	iShares MSCI Germany Index ETF
EWH	iShares MSCI Hong Kong Index ETF
EWJ	iShares MSCI Japan Index ETF
EWT	iShares MSCI Taiwan Index ETF
EWV	ProShares UltraShort MSCI Japan ETF
EWZ	iShares MSCI Brazil Index ETF
FARCE	Faithful annual rebalancing of common ETFs
FTSE	Financial Times and London Stock Exchange
FX	Foreign exchange
FXI	iShares FTSE China 25 Index Fund ETF
FXP	ProShares UltraShort FTSE China 25 ETF
GBP	British pound
GLD	SPDR Gold Trust ETF
GTC	Good until cancelled
HELOC	Home equity line of credit
HKD	Hong Kong dollar
IB	Interactive Brokers
IRA	Individual Retirement Account

IWM	iShares Russell 2000 Index ETF
JO	iPath DJ-UBS Coffee TR Sub-Idx ETN
JPY	Japanese yen
MAR	Managed Account Reports
MOO	Market Vectors Agribusiness ETF
MSCI	Morgan Stanley Capital International
NASDAQ	National Association of Securities Dealers Automated Quotation System
NLV	Net Liquidation Value
NYSE	New York Stock Exchange
NZD	New Zealand dollar
PALL	Physical Palladium Shares ETF
PPLT	Physical Platinum Shares ETF
PSQ	ProShares Short QQQ ETF
QID	ProShares UltraShort QQQ ETF
QQQ	PowerShares QQQ ETF
RSX	Market Vectors Russia ETF
RWM	ProShares Short Russell2000 ETF
SEK	Swedish krona
SH	ProShares Short S&P500 ETF
SKF	ProShares UltraShort Financials ETF
SLV	iShares Silver Trust ETF
SPY	SPDR S&P 500 ETF
TBT	ProShares UltraShort 20+ Year Treasury ETF

TIP	iShares Barclays TIPS Bond ETF
TIPS	Treasury inflation-protected securities
TLT	iShares Barclays 20+ Year Treasury Bond ETF
TWS	Trader Workstation
UGL	ProShares Ultra Gold ETF
UNG	United States Natural Gas ETF
US	United States
USD	US dollar
USO	United States Oil ETF
UUP	PowerShares DB US Dollar Index Bullish ETF
XLE	Energy Select Sector SPDR ETF
XLF	Financial Select Sector SPDR ETF

Introduction

Paper money eventually returns to its intrinsic value—zero.

—Voltaire

I've read a lot of trading, investing, and finance books over the years. One thing that really annoys me is reading the first third of the book and not learning anything new. Or realizing that the author has a completely different philosophy than I do on the subject, so I can't really get any benefit from the book. So I want to be sure with this book that you know exactly what you're getting before you spend time and money to understand my message.

For this reason it's easier to describe who this book is for, from a personal finance point of view, and let you decide whether you fit the profile. Then I'll briefly describe what the book is designed to help you with.

First, and most important, to benefit from the advice and techniques in this book, you need to be financially stable. I call this "financial fitness," and Chapter 1 deals with exactly what this means. Basically, you should have monthly net income that is greater than monthly fixed expenses (i.e., you should be cash flow positive). You also must have assets that are worth more than current liabilities (positive net worth).

If you're not financially fit (or close to it), then the three-step method this book describes will not be of much use to you. In this case I suggest you read some of the books on personal finances listed in Appendix A of this book, or check out the "Protect your Wealth from Inflation" page on my web site, at http://pmkingtrading.com. Only return to this book when you have achieved financial fitness.

Assuming that you do fit the description of financial fitness, then I'd like to explain what the rest of the book contains so you realize just how much you need this book! The book's title has three main words in it that should be big clues to what the book is about.

The words are:

- Protect
- Wealth
- Inflation

Let's deal with them in order.

Protect

Protection is not about generating a massive return really quickly. It's about the other side of the coin: preserving the assets that you already have and making sure you can more easily weather any financial storms that inevitably come along. For this reason, the first step in this book is about how to manage an emergency fund that can keep you afloat financially if you lose your primary income, have a large uninsured expense to deal with, or experience any other financial emergency. The important idea is that you need to manage your emergency fund in a way that will not be adversely affected by interest rates or other factors that are out of your control, like government monetary and fiscal policy.

A key concept in this book is that risk and return go hand in hand. It's very important that you think about the risk side of the equation first, and then make sure you're getting paid for that risk with a decent return. However, risk can be hidden in some unusual places. For example, if you put cash into a savings account paying an interest rate that is less than the current rate of inflation, then even though the dollar value of the account may be insured so it's "risk-free," you're still losing purchasing power every single day. Eventually, the money in the account that could, say, purchase six months worth of products and services when you put the cash in there, may only buy six weeks worth when you need it. How is that risk-free?

Chapter 2 explains the problem of inflation in detail. This is then followed up by Chapter 3, which outlines step one of my three-step method: how to protect the purchasing power of your emergency fund so it's still worth something when you need it.

Wealth

The second important word in the title is *wealth*, which is what you want to protect. Obviously, if you don't have any wealth to protect because your net worth (current assets minus current liabilities) is negative, then this book is not for you. If you do have a positive personal balance sheet because your monthly income is greater than your monthly expenses, then it's a good idea to have a plan for protecting and increasing the value of your working capital (funds that are not earmarked for emergencies but are not being used for investments).

Chapter 4 deals with how to effectively manage your savings and working capital regardless what the prevailing interest-rate and inflation environments are.

Once you are managing your emergency fund and working capital effectively, then further surplus income and assets can be put to use generating a satisfactory risk-adjusted return in investment accounts. Chapter 5 deals with how to manage investment accounts effectively by controlling risk, and then getting paid a decent return for the risk you are taking. Here's a small hint: traditional investment management techniques do not do this effectively at all. As you will learn, you must change your approach to avoid future disappointment. Buy-and-hold, dollar cost averaging, and other traditional financial management techniques just don't work very well. In this section of the book I'll describe in detail how to manage your investment account in a straightforward but sophisticated way to maximize your risk-adjusted return, and I'll also demonstrate how this approach provides a significantly better result than traditional portfolio management methods.

Inflation

Inflation is the last word in the title and is the main focus of the book. What does your wealth need protection from? Price inflation. As I mentioned earlier in this Introduction, Chapter 2 describes the problem of inflation in detail, but in terms that anyone can understand. Mitigating the effects of inflation forms the backdrop for each of the subsequent chapters.

I'm not formally trained in economics (thankfully) and I don't subscribe to any particular economic theory or policy. But I do have a great deal of experience helping people protect their portfolios from the losses that might otherwise occur when they stand by and watch inflation eat away at cash and investments. I just want everyone to understand why inflation is inevitable, what practical effect this has on your wealth, and how to do something about it so it doesn't end up significantly hurting your personal finances.

Chapter 6 is a summary of everything covered in the book and can be used to jog your memory as you continue to implement the three-step plan—a plan that helps you to effectively manage your money in three key areas:

- Emergency fund
- Savings
- Investments

In Summary

To sum up, this book is for individuals or families that are financially fit, have some wealth to protect, and need to effectively manage an emergency fund, savings and working capital, and investment accounts. The book describes a comprehensive but easy-to-understand step-by-step process you can follow to maximize your chances of success and minimize risk, and also help protect your assets from being ravaged by price inflation.

I wish you all success with your endeavors to protect your wealth from the ravages of inflation with the help of this book. Please send questions and comments to me via the contact page on http://pmkingtrading.com.

Financial Fitness

What Does It Mean to Be Financially Fit?

In the introduction, I mentioned that this book was intended for people who are already financially fit and therefore have income and assets that need protecting from inflation (and from the grasping clutches of the financial industry). This chapter describes exactly what being financially fit means, so that it's clear what shape your finances need to be in to benefit most from the information in the rest of the book.

Think of your personal finances as akin to owning a small business. You have income and expenses, and assets and liabilities, and whether the business is healthy or not is a simple matter of mathematics. If you can add and subtract, then you can work out whether you're financially fit or a debt-ridden disaster (or somewhere in between).

There are two important views of your finances that need to be considered. These are:

- Balance sheet
- Cash flow statement

Let's deal with each one in turn.

Balance Sheet

The balance sheet is simply a list of your current assets and liabilities. Assets are things that have a market value, such as a home, a car (that you own rather than lease), cash in a checking account, shares in a public listed company, and so on. Liabilities are things you owe to someone else. These include such things as your credit card balance, a personal loan, or a mortgage. Your net worth is simply the current value of your assets minus the current value of your liabilities. If this number is positive, then you're financially fit (i.e., you have a positive net worth). If the number is negative, then you're not financially fit. The bigger this number is, assuming it's positive, the fitter your finances are.

Not sure where you fit in? Following are some examples of people who are financially unhealthy, on the borderline, and financially fit. Each includes a balance sheet typical of those in the category.

Mr. and Mrs. Unfit

Mr. and Mrs. Unfit live in "affluent" suburbia. They have a lovely house that cost them $300,000 ten years ago. They refinanced their mortgage and added a second mortgage and a line of credit when house prices skyrocketed in their area five years ago. They used the cash for major renovations and a Caribbean vacation. Unfortunately, the housing bubble burst shortly after that, and the current market value of their house is only $250,000. However, they have $310,000 of outstanding debt secured on it. Thus, they are "underwater," with negative equity. They could not afford to move even if they wanted to.

They still take at least one expensive vacation per year and like to buy the latest electronic gadgets and designer clothes. Both Mr. and Mrs. Unfit have good jobs. Mr. Unfit receives a decent bonus each year that is normally at least 25% of his base salary. Unfortunately, Mr. Unfit's expected bonus is normally spent well before the end of the year. That's because they keep increasing their credit card balances and applying for new credit cards with low introductory rates. They are hoping house prices will run back up so they can sell for a profit and move closer to their aging parents.

But housing prices haven't budged. Worse, monthly expenses always seem to increase to use up all available cash (and then some). That in turn means they can't pay off credit card balances, and the checking account always seems to end up close to zero before the end of the month. If either of the Unfits loses their job, or they don't receive that nice bonus one year, this family cannot pay its monthly ex-

penses and has no reserves to survive even a small hiatus in income. *If interest rates rise significantly, they will be unable to meet their debt payments and will likely default and lose their home. They are only a couple of paychecks away from financial disaster and the situation is getting worse every month. Here is a balance sheet for the Unfits:*

Mr. and Mrs. Unfit's Balance Sheet

Assets

Primary residence market value	$250,000
Checking account	$2,000
Savings account	$1,000

Liabilities

First mortgage	$240,000
Second mortgage	$50,000
HELOC	$20,000
Credit card 1	$5,000
Credit card 2	$2,500
Credit card 3	$1,000

Net worth	–$65,500

Miss Borderline

Miss Borderline rents a small apartment in a metropolitan area. She went to college, graduated in computer programming, and currently works for a major software company. She saves a little each month and contributes to her company retirement plan, but her outstanding student loan balance is about the same size as her total assets, so she actually has very little net worth. She tries to keep expenses low and manages to pay off her credit cards monthly. She can't really afford a vacation or expensive clothes without increasing her credit card balances. Her savings account would not support her for very long at all if she lost her job, and she would have to go back to living with her parents if that happened. She is not getting financially worse off every month, but is still living paycheck to paycheck and can't seem to get ahead. Here is Miss Borderline's balance sheet:

Miss Borderline's Balance Sheet	
Assets	
Checking account	$1,000
Savings account	$600
Investment account	$5,000
Retirement account	$10,000
Liabilities	
Student loan	$16,000
Net worth	**$600**

Mr. and Mrs. Fit

Mr. and Mrs. Fit live in an area similar to the one Mr. and Mrs. Unfit live in. However, when the price of houses in their area went up and up, they did not refinance their mortgage, add a second mortgage, or add a home equity line of credit (HELOC). They simply refinanced their existing mortgage at a lower interest rate. They even kept their monthly payments the same in order to pay off the loan principal quicker. Their mortgage (which is their only current liability) should be paid off at least five years earlier than scheduled, saving them many thousands of dollars in interest payments. They have consistently kept monthly expenses lower than current income so that spare cash has accumulated in the checking account. Any excess cash gets transferred to a savings account on a monthly basis.

Mr. Fit contributes to his company retirement plan. His employer makes matching contributions, which he views as "free money." He is concerned about the risk he is taking in the retirement account, since he has observed losses greater than 50% at some points—notably in 2008—since he started contributing to it more than ten years ago.

With the money in their checking and savings accounts, Mr. and Mrs. Fit could easily pay their current expenses for ten months. If they cut these expenses down during such an "emergency" period, they could more than double this length of time to two years. They feel relatively secure with an emergency cash cushion of this size.

In addition to working as a mechanical engineer, Mr. Fit also patented an idea that was licensed by a manufacturing company that pays him an annual fee. Mrs. Fit has published several novels that generate monthly royalties. Although the Fit family is financially healthy and has both a positive net worth and a positive monthly cash flow statement, the Fits are still concerned about their financial future.

Some of the things that they worry about are that expenses could increase significantly during an inflationary environment, their retirement account balances could decrease significantly just when they need their retirement money the most, and the purchasing power of their emergency cash could be significantly diminished due to inflation. Moreover, since all their income and assets are in US dollars, they wonder what will happen if there is a significant weakening of the dollar relative to other major world currencies, which could cause expenses to rise much faster than their income. Here is a balance sheet for the Fits:

Mr. and Mrs. Fit's Balance Sheet

Assets	
Primary residence market value	$250,000
Checking account	$10,000
Savings account	$50,000
Investment account	$10,000
Retirement account	$250,000
Liabilities	
First mortgage	$200,000
Net worth	**$370,000**

Do you see yourself in one of these examples? If Mr. and Mrs. Unfit comes uncomfortably close to your situation, you have some work to do before this book will be of the highest value to you. Keep reading the next few pages, however, for a few tips on how to gain control of your financial future. If you are more like Miss Borderline, you're on the right track and should become fit if you continue to pay off your debts and find a way to save. Keep reading for some ideas on how to increase your income and make the day you reach fitness come sooner. And if you're like Mr. and Mrs. Fit, this book is for you.

There are only two ways to improve your balance sheet:

1. Increase assets.

2. Decrease liabilities.

Since the market value of most assets is not under your direct control, it's difficult to do anything about option 1. Therefore, the single best way to improve your balance sheet is simply to reduce liabilities. Pay down credit card debt, pay down mortgages, and pay off loans. Obviously, the cash to reduce the size of liabilities has to come from somewhere, and this brings us to the other important view of financial fitness: your cash flow statement.

Cash Flow Statement

Your personal cash flow statement is simply a list of income and expenses over some time period, typically monthly. Your net cash flow is easily calculated as total income minus total expenses. Again, if this number is positive, then you're financially fit. If it's negative, then you're not. And if it's close to zero, then you're borderline. Being borderline is an issue, because any small decrease in income or small increase in expenses can tip you over the edge financially.

It's important to note here that some items that appear on your balance sheet as assets may conversely appear on your cash flow statement generating expense line items. For example, your home does have a market value and is counted as an asset if you own rather than rent it, but from a cash flow point of view it will generate many (normally significant) expense items, such as mortgage interest payments, property tax, maintenance expenses, insurance, and so on. This is why it's important to view your finances from both a balance sheet and a cash flow point of view. You can't be financially fit if you have a positive net worth but negative cash flow—at some point the negative cash flow will eat up all your assets and turn your net worth negative as well.

Following are a few typical examples of financially unhealthy, borderline, and financially fit monthly income statement scenarios.

Mr. and Mrs. Unfit's Monthly Cash Flow

Income

Salary income 1	$3,125
Salary income 2	$1,500
Annual bonus (divided by 12)	$1,000

Expenses

Debt payments	$1,200
Other normal monthly expenses	$4,500
Net monthly cash flow	–$75

Miss Borderline's Monthly Cash Flow

Income

Salary income	$3,000

Expenses

Debt payments	$150
Other normal monthly expenses	$2,750
Net monthly cash flow	**$100**

Mr. and Mrs. Fit's Monthly Cash Flow

Income

Salary income	$4,000
Royalty income	$1,500
License income	$1,000

Expenses

Debt payments	$800
Other normal monthly expenses	$4,500
Net monthly cash flow	**$1,200**

Just as with your balance sheet, there are only two things you can do to improve your cash flow:

1. Increase income.

2. Reduce expenses.

Again, similar to the problem of not being able to easily increase the value of assets, most people are already earning the maximum income they can right now. So the only practical way to improve cash flow is to reduce expenses.

Increasing Income: An Alternative View

Let's take a quick detour. What follows may prove liberating for you and help you achieve—or extend—your financial fitness.

Not all income is created equal. In my view, "selling your time for money" (which is the most common income type) is actually the least desirable. Most people would be much better off if they at least recognized that there are better ways to produce income that are scalable, passive, repeatable, and recurring. Spending some of your time thinking about ways to make money that do not involve directly selling your time would be very beneficial to your financial health. Let's look at this in more detail.

If selling your time for money is the least desirable form of income, what's the most desirable? It has to do with the characteristics of the income itself. More desirable income has some, if not all, of the following characteristics:

- Passive
- Scalable
- Repeatable
- Recurring

Passive income is income that is earned whether you do anything or not. The interest you earn on your checking account balance is passive—the bank applies it automatically every month whether you ask it to or not. Unfortunately, this kind of passive income is typically the only passive income most people earn, and it's a very inefficient form of passive income. What would your checking account balance have to be so that the monthly interest earned paid all your current monthly expenses? The answer is typically "a very big number" and not a practical solution at as far as improving your financial health goes.

Scalable income is income that can grow bigger without a corresponding growth in time or effort or expenses. This is exactly the opposite of time-for-money income. If you get paid $25 per hour on average for doing something, the only way to increase your income is to work more hours. To earn an extra hour of pay you have to do an extra hour of work. Because there are only so many hours in the day and weeks in the year that you can work, this type of income just isn't scalable. Contrast this with building a web-based service that people pay to subscribe to. If it's designed correctly, each incremental subscriber does not significantly increase the operating cost of the service, yet it results in more income.

Repeatable income is income that you can earn multiple times for the same piece of work. A good example of this is writing and publishing a book. You do the work once but receive income in the form of a royalty every time a copy is sold. Try getting your employer to pay you again for the work you did yesterday. You'll discover that most of the work you're doing right now is only going to get you paid once.

Recurring income is income that keeps coming in on a regular periodic basis. An example of this would be a licensing payment you receive from a patent you filed and that a manufacturing company is using as a basis for a product they are producing. You would receive a recurring payment for the entire period of the license contract.

Some kinds of income incorporate all of the above characteristics, some only one or two, but in all cases any income that incorporates any of the above characteristics is better for your financial health than time-for-money income. It's essential that any financial plan includes some ideas and a time-frame for reducing your dependence on time-for-money income and increasing the other types accordingly. If you can achieve a situation where passive income is greater than monthly expenses, then you are financially free and can spend your time doing what you want to do, not what you need to do to make enough money to pay your monthly expenses.

Reducing Expenses: An Alternative View

If increasing income isn't viable right now, again, you're left with only one option to improve cash flow: reducing expenses. It's important to point out that reducing expenses isn't a very interesting subject to most people, and it's not hard to understand why. "Just spend less" equates to "reduce quality of life." That in turn leads to being less happy and ultimately actually spending more to try to make yourself feel better about wasting one-third of your life working for someone else doing something you wouldn't do if you weren't being paid for it. Again, it's beyond the scope of this book to go into detail about why it's better to focus on option 1, increasing income (ideally something other than employee-based income), but it is worth explaining why there are no "mandatory expenses" in my view of personal finances, and how that can help you improve your cash flow.

I'm sure you've seen the expense classifications in most personal finance management systems—they're typically split into mandatory and discretionary expenses. Most financial advisors will then get you to concentrate on the discretionary expenses (all the fun stuff you actually want to spend money on) and reduce them until your cash flow statement looks better.

But you will hate your pauper's lifestyle and simply abandon the plan. My view is that *there are no mandatory expenses.* All expenses are directly based on choices you have made about your lifestyle, where you live, what kind of car you drive, where your kids go to school, and so on.

If you're living a financial nightmare in which your income is tiny and your expenses are huge, it's simply because of the choices *you* have made. This can be a scary thought at first. You might think, "Why would I choose to create my own financial nightmare?" But once you get past the fear, it can be liberating. The simple truth is that if your financial situation is a direct result of your own choices, then *you are in control.* All you have to do to improve the situation is *make better choices.*

This means that all expenses are discretionary. If you don't want to pay property tax, then either rent a home or move to a state that has no property tax. If you don't want a huge grocery bill each month, stop choosing food that can't be grown locally or isn't in season, and grow some of your own produce. If you want to reduce your car expenses, don't simply lease a new vehicle you can't afford to buy when your current lease expires. Instead, buy a used car for cash.

For most people, renting a home would be a much better financial decision than owning one. You would exchange a relatively large variable expense (mortgage interest, maintenance costs, etc.)—based on a volatile and illiquid asset—for a smaller, fixed monthly expense. If your circumstances change and you need to reduce expenses, it's much easier and less costly to move to a cheaper rental than to try to sell a house and buy another one.

The main point is that all your current expenses are fair game when it comes to changing your financial situation, and not really mandatory or fixed—if you have the will to become cash flow positive, then all it takes is a little ingenuity and a willingness to change the choices you've made.

In Summary

In summary, it's essential to be financially healthy before any of the rest of the ideas and methods in this book will be of use to you. Being financially healthy means two things:

1. Having a positive balance sheet

2. Having a net positive monthly cash flow

If neither of these applies to you, then the best thing you can do is stop reading this book and put a plan together that addresses both the issues over a reasonable period of time (one to five years is feasible for most people, depending on how bad the current situation really is). The sooner you start doing something about your financial situation, the quicker it will be fixed. Then you will have some cash reserves and assets you want to protect and grow using the rest of the techniques presented in this book.

Inflation: What's the Problem?

If Your Finances Are Fit, Why Should You Worry?

If you have read this far, then I'm going to make an assumption: your finances look similar to Mr. and Mrs. Fit's, or you have a detailed plan in place to achieve that kind of financial fitness over the next few years. At this point you may be thinking to yourself, "If my finances looked like Mr. and Mrs. Fit's, then I wouldn't have a problem!" You'd be right—you wouldn't have *a* problem, you'd have *three* major problems:

- What will I do if my monthly expenses rise significantly due to price inflation but my cash reserves don't increase in value by the same amount due to a low-interest-rate environment?
- What will I do if my savings don't even generate a positive real rate of return due to interest rates being lower than the prevailing inflation rate?

- What will I do if my retirement or investment account loses significant value just before I need it, or it doesn't generate a reasonable risk-adjusted return that's greater than inflation rates?

Table 2-1 shows the three types of capital and what the objectives are for each. It's useful to think of your cash assets as being in one of the following "buckets":

- An emergency fund, in which the objective is to pay fixed expenses for a number of months if you lose your main source of income
- Savings accounts, where the objective is to make a positive real rate of return with low or zero risk of losing value on funds you intend to use over the medium term (say, in the next few years)
- Investment accounts, where the objective is to generate a good risk-adjusted rate of return on capital that you do not need to use for a number of years (in retirement, for example)

Table 2-1. Types of capital and the objectives for each.

Capital	Risk Level	Objective
Emergency fund	None	Maintain purchasing power
Savings	Low	Positive real rate of return
Investments	Medium	Good risk-adjusted return

Table 2-2 shows the typical implementation for each type of capital and what the problems associated with that implementation are.

Table 2-2. The typical implementations of capital and the problems associated with each one.

Capital	Typical Implementation	Problems in Implementation
Emergency fund	Checking account, cash, Treasury inflation-protected securities (TIPS)	Diminished purchasing power due to inflation
Savings	Saving account, money market fund, certificates of deposit (CDs)	Negative real rate of return due to interest rates lower than inflation; single-currency volatility
Investments	Diversified equity and bond portfolio with periodic rebalancing	Poor or negative return; unmanaged risk

The rest of this book is about how to deal with these specific problems. It will address each of them in turn. The remainder of this chapter gives a detailed explanation of exactly what the problems are, and how they manifest themselves in our personal finances.

The Problem of Reduced Purchasing Power and Negative Real Interest Rates

It's a good idea to maintain an emergency fund designed to pay expenses for 6 to 12 months in the event you lose your job or primary income. Typically, emergency funds will simply be held in your checking account, or even in $100 bills stuffed under your mattress. If you are a little more sophisticated, you may have even had the foresight to put this money into an investment that is supposed to be protected from inflation. These include the Treasury Inflation Protected Security exchange-traded fund (ETF), which uses the market symbol TIP, and TIPS purchased directly from the US Treasury.

Unfortunately, all of these solutions face one significant problem: inflation. First let's define exactly what we mean by "inflation." In the context of this book, inflation simply means that the price of specific products and services goes up each month. This means that consuming the exact same goods and services you did last month will cost you more (in your domestic currency) this month.

Figure 2-1 shows the "official" numbers for price inflation using the Consumer Price Index for All Urban Consumers (CPI-U) from 2004 to 2011. I call these the official numbers because this is the measure of inflation that government obligations (like TIPS) are linked to.

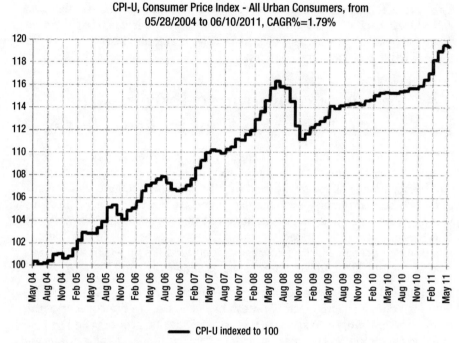

Figure 2-1. CPI-U, May 2004 to June 2011

As you can see, this inflation measure definitely has an upward trend, and the compound annual growth rate (CAGR) is 1.79%. In other words, according to the CPI-U, prices went up 1.79% per year on average during this period. If you had kept your emergency fund in cash, it would have lost 1.79% of its purchasing power each year. Put another way, every $100 in expenses at the start of the period would have risen to $119 at the end.

This may not seem like such a big deal for a seven-year period. However, there are two significant issues here:

- Finding a risk-free investment that simply keeps pace with "official" inflation is not straightforward.
- The CPI-U understates your personal real rate of inflation by a significant amount.

The Treasury Inflation Protected Security ETF (trading symbol TIP) is designed to track the changes in the CPI-U and therefore provide a return that matches inflation. Figure 2-2 shows the performance of TIP over the same time period as the CPI-U from Figure 2-1.

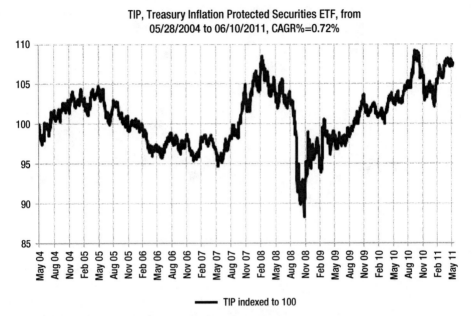

Figure 2-2. Return on investment in TIP, May 2004 to June 2011

As you can see, the CAGR is 0.72%, which is significantly lower than the annual increase in the CPI-U. This means that even if the CPI-U were representative of your actual increase in monthly expenses due to inflation, investing in TIP would not provide enough return to maintain the purchasing power of your emergency fund. You could invest in TIPS directly, but they require you to pay federal taxes on the interest every year and capital gains when the bonds mature, so unless you're in the zero percent tax bracket for federal taxes, the after-tax returns, again, do not match the CPI-U.

An alternative would be to invest in an ETF that buys Treasury bonds like TLT. Figure 2-3 shows the performance of this investment over the same period.

Figure 2-3. Return on investment in TLT, June 2004 to June 2011

The performance is slightly better than TIP, but still worse than the CPI-U increases.

But here's the kicker: I'm sure if you go back and look at your personal expenses over this same period, you'll find that they will probably have increased significantly more than 1.79% per year. Figure 2-4, which shows the increase in a basket of various commodities over the same period, indicates how much "real" prices have increased.[1]

---

[1] The commodities used were cocoa, coffee, corn, heating oil, oats, crude oil, rice, soybeans, sugar, and wheat.

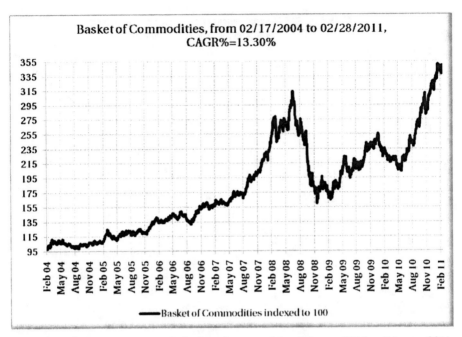

Figure 2-4. Increase in prices of a basket of commodities, February 2004 to February 2011

This is a much more representative estimation of real, in-your-wallet price inflation over the same period, and equates to about 1% inflation *per month* rather than *per year* over this period.

Figure 2-5 shows how much the Fit family's monthly living expenses would increase over five years (from the current $4,500 per month) if prices went up (inflated) by an average of only 1.18% per month.

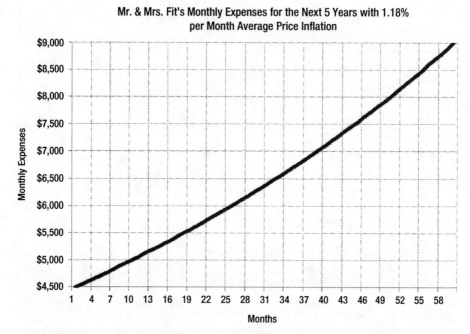

Figure 2-5. The Fits' monthly expenses with 1.18% per month price inflation.

As you can see in Figure 2-5, monthly living expenses, not including debt payments, would double from $4,500 to $9,000 over five years with price increases of 1.18% per month. Incidentally, I cheated when I created this chart by using the spreadsheet's "what-if" analysis to set the monthly increase so that expenses exactly doubled over the ten-year period. What I really wanted to demonstrate is how a seemingly low monthly increase of just over 1% can turn into a significant increase in expenses over time due to the power of compounding (working against you in this case).

If the Fits do nothing about this problem, then their "emergency fund"—the $60,000 sitting in their checking and savings accounts—will only cover expenses for just over 6 months in 5 years time, in contrast to the 12 months that it covers right now.

Yes, the Fits could continue to add to the emergency fund with spare cash every month, assuming that their income rises accordingly, but this is addressing the symptoms of the problem, not the root cause.

You may be thinking, "How could the government's official figures be so far off? Are you sure the CPI is so seriously flawed?" It's a fair question and deserves a detailed answer. But first, let me ask you a few questions:

- Why is it that actual monthly expenses showing up on your pay-check, credit card statement, and checking account statement seem to go up much more than the "official" figures presented in the CPI?
- If the CPI says that inflation for last year was at 2%, but your health insurance premiums just went up 10% over the same period, which is the best number to use as a measure of your personal price inflation rate?
- If the monthly meal in your favorite restaurant costs 10% more than it did just a few months ago, are you content with skipping the expensive bottle of wine, or ordering something cheaper to keep the cost increase down to a number similar to the CPI?
- Are you happy to eat less because the manufacturer of the canned soup you like has kept the price the same but reduced the size of the can, or would you prefer to recognize this as another form of price inflation and understand that consuming as much soup as you did last month will cost you more?
- How are things at the gas pump these days?
- Have you recently had to reduce coverage on an insurance policy just to keep the premiums under control?

I have to make it clear that I'm not an economist, I haven't studied economic theory, and I don't know what the flaws are in various economic models or theories. I only care about the practical implications of what happens in the real world, and what we can all do to attempt to insulate ourselves from the detrimental effects of decisions beyond our control.

Although this book will talk about why the government measures of inflation typically understate real price increases and why government fiscal and monetary policy will always cause price inflation, it is not concerned with whether this is right or wrong and whether it's possible to fix it. Rather, it is concerned with accepting the situation and presenting solutions to prevent it from becoming a problem *for your personal financial situation*. It doesn't really matter what the CPI says, or what the government does to the US dollar; what really matters is that your emergency fund maintains its purchasing power so that it will pay for the same amount of monthly products and services it does today, but in 10, 20, or 50 years time.

Why Inflation Is Inevitable

Today, there are no major currencies that are tied to anything physical in the real world. They are all "fiat" currencies that exist (and have perceived value) simply by the word and rules of the government that creates them. *Fiat* means "by decree." Therefore there is no practical constraint on the amount of these currency units that can be created by the government and the banking system because currencies are no longer tied to a physical commodity (as they were when "the gold standard" existed).

The actual supply (total quantity) of currency units that exists is determined by two main factors:

- Fractional-reserve banking rules
- Government fiscal and monetary policy

Of course, neither you and I—nor any state or local government—can create dollars, pounds, euros, or any other currency. That is called counterfeiting, and is illegal and normally punished severely. However, when you go to the bank for a mortgage to buy a house, the dollars for the loan are simply created where none existed before due to the magic (or alchemy if you prefer) of fractional-reserve banking.

Here's what that means. If a bank has $1 in reserves—say, money you just deposited in your checking account—it is allowed to loan out about $10. The $9 in addition to the actual $1 it has in reserves is created in a computer somewhere and represents brand new dollars that did not exist before you borrowed them. This is how loose credit policies and low interest rates cause more people to take out loans, which in turn increases the actual supply of money in circulation. If economic activity—that is, the amount of products and services produced in the economy—increases more slowly than the money supply, then prices will go up. There is more cash chasing the same amount of products and services.

The other factor that affects the money supply directly is government fiscal policy. When the government of a country that has a fiat currency wants to increase its spending, it has three main choices:

1. Create an environment where the economy grows, which in turn means business revenue and employee salaries grow, which in turn means tax revenue grows, and the government can grow along with it.

2. Increase tax rates so that tax revenue grows at the required pace even if the economy is not growing.

3. Simply increase budgets and create some new currency units to cover the increased spending.

Most governments increase spending relentlessly, but the economy is cyclical. That means option 1, growing with the economy, is not going to be available all the time. Also, growing only at the pace of the economy creates a built-in budget constraint. Such "organic" growth is not fast enough for politicians who want to provide ever more services and benefits for constituents.

Option 2 is a very visible and very unpopular solution to the government's constant growth problem. If a government simply raised taxes to pay for increased spending, it would soon be voted out of office. So this option is hardly ever chosen. This is also compounded by the fact that citizens want lots of government services but are not prepared to pay for them with higher taxes. We can't simply blame the politicians.

Option 3 solves the problem by "hiding" the increased spending by creating more currency units. In this way, a government can grow independently of downturns in the economic cycle, it doesn't have to visibly raise taxes, and the consequences of its actions are not immediately apparent to the general public. Unfortunately, this approach causes a devaluation of the currency, which everyone eventually experiences in the form of rising prices— which is just another way of saying that the purchasing power of the currency you have now is going down as you read this sentence. One solution is to simply spend every cent you can get your hands on right now since it's going to buy less tomorrow. But that's not a very practical solution for most fiscally responsible people who want to plan for a prosperous rather than bankrupt future.

It is possible for this to all work out fine. If the economy happens to start growing at a rate similar to the increase in the money supply, then inflation will not get out of control, and all the economists and government officials will say, "Hey, look, that worked and everything is OK now." However, what if the economy does not start to grow for a while, but the money supply continues to be increased to fund expensive government programs and more federal employees? Or what if it grows more slowly than the money supply? Then we will have significant inflation. Your standard of living will go down because prices will go up—a lot. I'm afraid it's almost inevitable. I'm sure you don't want to leave your financial future to chance and the belief that the government always knows what it is doing.

Here's a simple explanation of how inflation comes about. Say a rich relative suddenly added $1 million to your bank account. You'd be really happy, right? You would immediately have significant free cash (compared to the average American anyway) and be able to purchase basically any product or service you wanted. But what if the relative were so rich and generous that he added $1 million to every US checking account? All that would happen then would be that the price of everything would skyrocket. Everyone would have an extra $1 million dollars to compete for the same products and services that you want to purchase. More money chasing the same amount of products and services simply means prices have to go up, as they do whenever demand increases and supply doesn't keep up.

This book is not about the evils of government, how to fix the system, or why you should be angry or concerned about the situation. It's about practical measures you can take once you understand what's going on to make sure you are minimally impacted by the adverse effects of governmental fiscal or monetary policy, loose credit policies, low interest rates, and the resulting price inflation. So, now that you understand why inflation in a fiat-currency environment is very likely in the short term (and inevitable in the long term), you can do something to protect your wealth from the effects of it.

Drilling Down on the CPI

You may be thinking, "Why do the US government's inflation figures, published in the form of the CPI, usually show inflation in the low single digits for an entire year?" The CPI, which has a lot of its obligations linked to it (like federal employee pensions, Social Security payments, etc.), is supposed to represent real price inflation experienced by the general public. And while it has been showing low inflation for the last few years, the way the CPI is calculated (some would say manipulated) means that it does not accurately reflect real inflation.

A true and fair gauge of your personal cost of living index would cover two things:

- A basket of goods and services that represent *all the major expenses you personally incur*, including energy, food, housing, utilities, transportation, entertainment, education, medical care, taxes, and so forth.
- Complete consistency in the products and services that are included in your basket from year to year so the real true rate of price inflation can be easily observed and tracked.

Unfortunately, the CPI has three drawbacks as a measure of personal price inflation:

- It was not designed to be a true cost-of-living measure.[2]
- It uses a method called "hedonic quality adjustment" that adjusts the price of components in the index when they have to be replaced by products no longer available.
- The government has significant obligations linked to the CPI, which has a tendency to cause "improvements" or changes in the way the CPI is calculated to typically understate rather than overstate inflation.

Let's look at some specifics. An entry-level TV set used to cost $100, and now it costs $200. But the new model now has more ports on it to plug in electronic gadgets, and it has a higher-resolution screen. Nonetheless, the basic mathematical fact is that it now costs twice as much as it did before. However, in calculating the CPI, the government doesn't incorporate a doubling of the price of the TV set. Instead, the price increase is adjusted downward to reflect the increased quality (or utility) the consumer is receiving.

An even better example (or worse, depending on your point of view) is this one: when the federal government mandates use of ethanol, a gasoline additive designed to reduce pollution, this addition increases the price at the pump by, say, 10%. Does the gasoline component of the CPI go up by 10%? Nope. A hedonic quality adjustment is used to reduce the extent of the price increase due to the improved air quality consumers benefit from. The fact that your monthly outlay on gasoline just went up 10% does not show up in the CPI at all.[3]

Whether the way the CPI is calculated is right or wrong is not directly relevant. What really matters is this: by how much does it understate your personal cost of living index? How have historical modifications to the method affected the index as published? And how can you really maintain the purchasing power of your emergency funds by buying securities linked to the CPI-U?

Let's assume for a second that the CPI-U as published understates your personal cost-of-living index by 7%. This means that when the CPI-U says inflation is at 2% per year, your personal expenses are really going up by 9% per

---

[2] Quoting from the US Bureau of Labor Statistics web site, "The CPI frequently is called a cost-of-living index, but it differs in important ways from a complete cost-of-living measure." For much more information about the CPI, see www.bls.gov/cpi/cpifaq.htm.

[3] For more information about how changes in the method of calculation of the CPI and hedonic quality adjustments have consistently lead to understatements of inflation, see the free articles at www.shadowstats.com.

year. Since there's no security you can invest in that pays you a spread over the CPI-U of 7%, then it's irrelevant whether the CPI calculation is underestimating your personal inflation—what matters it that you understand the problem this causes for your emergency fund *and can do something about it.*

Chapter 3 is all about how to maintain the purchasing power of your emergency cash in an environment in which expenses are always rising. It contains practical advice and actions that you can take to protect yourself and your wealth.

Increases in the cost of personal monthly living expenses are not the only problem most people face with their finances. Another hidden risk that is often overlooked is the fact that all income and assets are normally denominated in a single domestic currency. The following section is a discussion of why this could end up being a big problem for you.

The Single-Currency "Problem"

Mr. and Mrs. Fit's finances may look great to you, but there are a couple of hidden problems: all their income and assets are in a single currency, US dollars. This is typical for most people I discuss finances with.

The two problems with this situation are:

- A negative real rate of return if interest rates are currently less than the rate of inflation
- Single-currency risk in the form of your domestic currency purchasing power relative to other major world currencies

As of April 2011, the average interest rate in the United States for a one-year CD was about 1.25%, and the annual increase of the CPI-U using the latest figures available is just over 2%. This means that the "real" interest rate on the CD is –0.75%. It's simply not worth buying a CD (or any other near-cash investment) if you're going to receive a negative real rate of return on it.

The other problem is single-currency risk. Figure 2-6 shows clearly why this is an issue. It's a chart of the US Dollar Index, an index composed of a basket of major currencies.[4] Again, it's indexed to 100 for comparison, and it shows how the "value" of the US dollar measured relative to other major world currencies has changed over the last ten years. The CAGR is –4.42%, which means that the dollar buys much less of those other currencies than

---

[4] These are the British pound, Canadian dollar, euro, Japanese yen, Swedish krona, and Swiss franc.

it did ten years ago. It starts off at 100 but ends up at about 62—about a 38% drop in value.

If you have all your assets in dollars, and all your future expenses are going to be in dollars, and you only want to purchase domestic products and services, then this is not much of a problem. However, what if you want to travel the world, or your children want to go to college in Asia, or you want to purchase a vacation or retirement home in Italy? Then it becomes a big deal if your huge stash of US dollars ends up with meager purchasing power when you need it.

Additionally, if the US dollar is significantly weakening vs. other major currencies, then if you don't own those other currencies, you are missing out on a good opportunity to generate a better return on your cash. If those other currencies are paying a positive real rate of interest while the US dollar is not, then you're missing out twice.

Figure 2-6. US Dollar Index, August 2001 to July 2011

Chapter 4 shows you exactly how to deal with this currency problem so you no longer have to worry about a significant weakening in your home currency, especially if you have current or planned future expenses that are not in your home currency, or savings sitting in an account making a negative real rate of return.

Who's in Charge, You or the Financial Industry?

If you've ever had an encounter with the financial industry, or watched any of the mainstream financial shows on TV, then I'm sure you will have heard some of the following statements more than once:

- You can't time the markets.
- Buying and holding a diversified portfolio of instruments is the only way to succeed in investing.
- Periodic rebalancing should be done so your portfolio doesn't get too heavily weighted in any one instrument, sector, or industry.
- You shouldn't sell if the price goes way down; you'll only lock in the losses and guarantee failure.
- "The market" will return 10% per year on average over long periods of time as long as you stick to the plan and stay 100% invested.
- Dollar cost averaging is an effective way to manage your investments.

I believe all of these statements are totally true, as long as you put one small phrase at the start of each one: "It's better for the financial industry if the customers believe that . . ."

Chapter 5 will explain how all of these "conventional wisdom" statements are the exact opposite of what's good for your investment portfolio, and how to manage your own investment capital simply and effectively.

Everything you generally hear about investing is from the point of view of the financial industry and what's best for it in terms of generating fees and commissions, rather than what's good for your portfolio or personal finances. It's important to note that I'm not talking about hedge funds or any financial setup where the portfolio manager's incentive is directly tied to performance and geared toward generating a good risk-adjusted return. I'm talking about situations where the company gets paid by fees based simply on asset value or commissions based on number of trades executed. If you've ever visited a financial advisor, the following narrative may sound very familiar to you.

Mr. and Mrs. Fit Visit a Broker/Advisor

Mr. and Mrs. Fit decide to visit a financial advisor to address some of the concerns Mr. Fit has about their finances. They take a recommendation from a friend who knows someone who visited Super Choice Asset Management, which has a branch in a nearby town.

They call up and arrange an appointment to see one of the advisors at SCAM, Mr. Sales. Mr. Sales is an employee of SCAM and receives a monthly allowance from the company, which is actually a loan against future commissions and fees Mr. Sales will generate by selling the company's financial products to customers like Mr. and Mrs. Fit.

After looking over Mr. and Mrs. Fit's financial picture, Mr. Sales is very pleased. He tells the Fits that they are in excellent financial shape but should not have most of their assets in cash, because they are generating virtually zero return. Mr. Sales recommends that the Fits open an account with his company, and tells them that he can put them into some TIPS (for a very reasonable fee). These, he says, will not only pay interest, but the principal will be adjusted over time based on the Bureau of Labor Statistics Consumer Price Index. Their savings will be protected from inflation.

Mr. Sales fails to mention that the Fits could buy the TIPS direct from the US Treasury if they wanted to, but then he would not receive any compensation for that advice. He's only doing his job, after all.

Mr. Sales also notes that the Fits have no professionally managed investment accounts that could be a source of funds in retirement. He recommends that they deposit the cash from their savings account into their new investment account at SCAM. SCAM has an excellent management program where, for a reasonable annual fee, experienced portfolio managers will expertly select mutual funds chosen from SCAM's wide choice. That will enable the Fits to maintain a diversified portfolio that will be rebalanced quarterly to keep the percentage allocation to each mutual fund exactly where it should be.

Once that's done, Mr. Sales could also help them move all their other current investment assets over to their SCAM account so that they would no longer be classed as a "small client," and would be eligible for a considerable saving in fees and other charges. Also, if they did this, then Mr. Sales would become their personal client manager and they could call him at any time to help with their finances or learn more about any of the numerous financial products and services his company offers to "clients of greater means."

There will be a fee for management of the account, of course, based on the value of assets in it, and there will also be fees for buying and selling the mutual funds in the account (which are listed in the rather thick prospectus for each fund that Mr.

Sales will give to the Fits), and commissions due if the Fits want to buy and sell securities in their own trading accounts. Mr. Sales doesn't normally recommend this last option, since the Fits will have access to the best portfolio managers in the industry right here at SCAM. "Why risk making a mistake and losing your hard-earned cash by 'gambling' on your own?" he asks.

Mr. Fit asks if they can invest in any foreign currencies or precious metals in the SCAM account, and Mr. Sales says that is not possible or recommended by his company—it's far too risky for most clients. He can, however talk to the Fits about some mutual funds that invest in gold-mining companies, and another one that is based on the US Dollar Index, which he believes is suitable if the Fits really want exposure to foreign currency exchange rates.

Mr. Sales also gravely notes that the Fits don't seem to have enough whole life insurance, buildings and contents insurance, auto insurance, disability insurance, or health insurance, and he would be pleased to help them deal with all their insurance needs. Another insurance product the Fits may be interested in would be a variable annuity—a great choice for a retirement account, in Mr. Sales's opinion.

The Fits leave the financial advisor with a heap of paperwork and a significant number of mutual fund prospectuses to review. But they don't really get any answers to their concerns about maintaining the purchasing power of their emergency cash, achieving a positive real rate of return on their savings, or making a good risk-adjusted return in their investment accounts.

All in all, they feel like they were just pitched a load of products and services that didn't exactly meet their needs and a few other ideas that were primarily designed to maximize the commission Mr. Sales would receive rather than improve the Fits' financial situation.

How the Market Has *Really* Done

Figure 2-7 shows exactly how the market has performed over a ten-year period, but using measures that no typical financial industry company will present to their customers. It shows the S&P 500, represented by the exchange-traded fund (ETF) SPY, indexed to 100 so you can compare it to the other charts presented in this chapter. As you can see, it starts off at 100, goes down to just above 60, goes back up to 120, goes down to about 55, and then finishes about where it started around 110.

The CAGR is 1.21% for this period, a long way from the 10% figure often informally stated as "typical" equity returns. The interesting statistics here show how much of a loss was suffered during this period (measured as the percentage change from the highest high to a subsequent low, called *drawdown [DD]*). In this case, it was 56.47%. So in order to have achieved a

1.21% annual growth rate, you would have had to have held on through a 56.47% drawdown in your portfolio. Dividing the CAGR by the maximum drawdown gives us the MAR (Managed Account Reports) ratio, which is named for the company that invented it. In this case, the MAR ratio is 0.021. This means that for every unit of risk (represented by the maximum drawdown from a high to a subsequent low as a percentage), the investment strategy would have paid you 0.021 units of reward per year. Put another way, for every $100 of risk you took, you got paid $1.21 per year. Does that sound like a good deal to you?

SPY S&P 500, from 08/13/2001 to 07/22/2011, CAGR%=1.21%, Maximum DD=56.47%, MAR=0.021

Figure 2-7. SPY S&P 500 investment return, August 2001 to July 2011. Here and throughout, MAR stands for Managed Account Reports ratio, and DD stands for drawdown.

In my experience, the MAR ratio needs to be at least 0.5 to represent a "sound investment." This means that, on average, you should have a CAGR percentage that is no less than half the maximum DD over the same period.

This is important because looking at return without quantifying the risk that's been taken to achieve the return (represented by DD in this case) is not representative of how an investment is performing. If I told you that I knew of an investing method that had returned 25% per year over the last ten years, would you be interested? Of course. Well, how would your feelings change if I told you that you would have to suffer a 99% drawdown of your capital at some point in order to achieve the 25% CAGR? I don't know of any sane person that would knowingly accept that level of risk to achieve a 25% per year return.

Another thing about Figure 2-7 is that it does not even take into account inflation eating away at your meager returns. If that had been included, it would mean that the CAGR was actually negative over the last ten years. You would have been taking all this risk and ending up with less purchasing power now than you had when you started.

If you've bought into the conventional wisdom that putting all your eggs in one basket at the start is not a good idea and that "dollar cost averaging" is the way to go, then the next chart may be an eye-opener for you. Dollar cost averaging means putting a certain amount of money into an investment on a periodic basis—say, monthly—to smooth out the market's volatility.

Figure 2-8 shows how an account would have performed if, instead of just buying the SPY at the start of the period, you had simply invested $1,000 per month and bought as many shares of SPY each month as that amount would purchase. (This chart does not include commission, so actual results would be worse than those shown.) As you can see, this technique does improve things slightly—the MAR has gone up from 0.021 to 0.028. Unfortunately the results are still very poor, and you still have to suffer a terrible 56% DD and only receive a tiny 1.60% CAGR.

Figure 2-8. SPY S&P 500 dollar cost averaging, August 2001 to July 2011

Right now you may be thinking, "Wait a minute, those charts don't include the periodic rebalancing of a diversified portfolio everyone tells us is the way to go," and you'd be right. That's where Figure 2-9 comes in. This shows how a $100,000 investment account would have performed since 2003 if it had been invested in the (typical) ETFs shown in Table 2-3.

Table 2-3. Typical ETF allocation.

ETF	Name	Allocation
SPY	S&P 500	50%
TLT	iShares Barclays 20 Year Treasuries	40%
EFA	iShares MSCI EAFE Index	10%

In the portfolio, SPY represent US equities, TLT represents US Treasury bonds, and EFA represents Europe, Australasia, and Far East equities.

The portfolio was rebalanced annually so that the percentage allocations were reset to the above values at the end of each year. I call this technique "faithful annual rebalancing of common ETFs," or FARCE for short. As you can see from the chart, this did improve results from the standard SPY portfolio, but they're not exactly stunning. CAGR has gone up to 1.67%, DD has been reduced to 35.15%, and the MAR ratio is now 0.047. This all means that the portfolio would have been worth just under $118,000 at the end of this period.

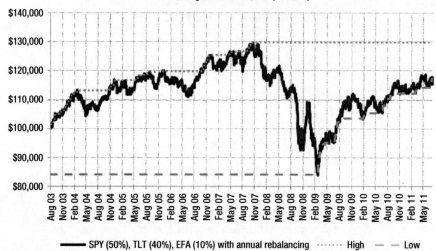

SPY (50%), TLT (40%), EFA (10%) with Annual Rebalancing,
Starting Value $100,000, 2% Annual Fee, from 08/14/2003 to
07/22/2011, CAGR%=1.67%, Maximum DD=35.15%, MAR=0.047,
Ending Value $117,991 (17.99%)

——— SPY (50%), TLT (40%), EFA (10%) with annual rebalancing ······· High — — Low

Figure 2-9. Annual rebalancing of a diversified portfolio, August 2003 to July 2011

The important thing to note is the shape of the graph when you compare it to the shape of the SPY graph in Figure 2-7 over the same period. It looks almost identical. All that has happened is that the diversification and periodic rebalancing has slightly increased the CAGR and slightly reduced the DD. This brings us to the serious flaw of "buy and hold with periodic rebalancing"—it only works *when the prices of all the instruments in your portfolio go up*. If you (or your financial advisor) can consistently only invest in things that always go up, then you'll be fine. (And please let me know who your advisor is—I'd like to invest with him.)

If you think about it, this makes intuitive sense. If you sell your big leaders (which have gone up and therefore now represent a bigger percentage of your portfolio than their original allocation) each year and use the proceeds to buy more of the laggards (which have gone up less), then you can only consistently make money if the price of everything is going up. There is only one instrument class that consistently goes up in real terms (which we'll get to in a moment), so the only conclusion that you can draw is that "buy and hold with periodic rebalancing" just doesn't work. If you use this method you'll be lucky to end up with what you started with (in absolute terms). However, the purchasing power of your account will be significantly diminished due to price inflation and currency weakening.

As an aside, periodic rebalancing is the exact opposite of two of the golden rules of trading, which are "Let your winners run" and "Cut your losers short." As a competent trader (rather than an investor), I know this (and also that markets don't always go in one direction). That's why I never use the principle of rebalancing in my investing.

This brings us on nicely to Figure 2-10. I mentioned previously that there is only one instrument class that generally goes up in real terms, and that is the class of physical commodities. Since commodities are priced in dollars—and as I've explained in this chapter, the purchasing power of dollars will generally decrease—we'd expect to see the "price" of commodities (such as gold in this example) increase in dollar terms over time. This is shown clearly in Figure 2-10. It shows the price of gold in dollars indexed to 100 (so you can compare it to the SPY chart in Figure 2-7) from September 1998 to April 2011.

I've included the same measures (CAGR, DD, and MAR) so you can clearly see how gold has performed. The CAGR is over 17%, but the maximum DD was under 30%. This means the MAR ratio was just under 0.6, which is a respectable ratio for any kind of investment method.

THE IMPORTANCE OF THE MAR RATIO

One significant problem most people have is an inability to effectively evaluate investment returns, especially from a comparative point of view. In other words, were the returns from investment A better or worse than those from investment B? And were either of them acceptable? The MAR ratio gives us a simple but effective measure of investment performance that should be the primary measure used to make financial decisions. Simply put, it is the CAGR divided by the maximum drawdown (DD) over the same period:

MAR = CAGR / DD

If an investment had a CAGR of 25% and a maximum drawdown during the same period of 50%, then the MAR ratio would be 25% / 50% = 0.5. This, in fact, would represent a relatively good risk-adjusted return, since risk and reward always go hand in hand, and the CAGR is earned every year, but the maximum drawdown is only suffered once. Calculating the MAR of any investment situation (even if you have to estimate the risk and return) is a useful exercise.

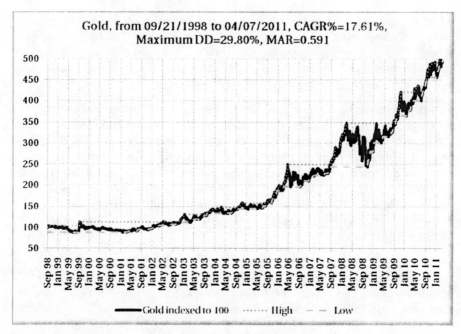

Figure 2-10. Gold return, September 1998 to April 2011

Note that if you take the currency out of the equation and show a ratio of commodity prices, then the graph will not generally go up. For example, on average, over a long period of time, 1 ounce of gold will be "worth" about 12 barrels of crude oil. Figure 2-10 is showing you the weakening of the currency (US dollars in this case), not the increase in value of the commodity.

Figure 2-11 shows the gold/oil ratio over the same time period. As you can see, the ratio is volatile, but oscillates around an average rather than showing a significant trend in either direction.

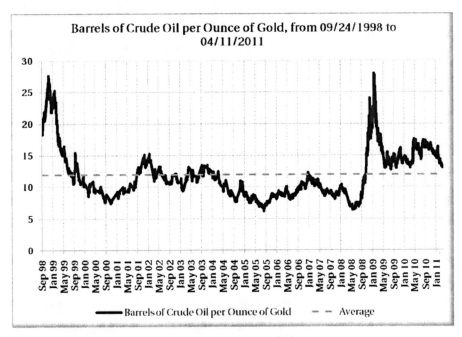

Figure 2-11. Gold/oil ratio, September 1998 to April 2011

It's fair to say that if you use traditional methods to manage your investment portfolio, then at best you'll end up where you started but with less purchasing power, and at worst you'll lose more than 50% of your investment. Chapter 5 presents a practical solution to this problem by detailing a way to achieve a much better risk-adjusted return in your investment accounts without having to become a full-time trader (and without having to pay anyone for the privilege of generating a terrible MAR ratio with your hard-earned cash).

In Summary

This chapter has explained the three major problems with an inflationary, negative real interest environment, even if your finances are otherwise fit.

These problems are:

- Loss of purchasing power of emergency cash due to price inflation and a negative real interest rate
- Relative weakness and negative real rate of interest of home currency compared to foreign currencies

- Poor risk-adjusted return on investments

The rest of this book presents practical and simple-but-elegant solutions to the three problems that anyone with a reasonable level of financial intelligence and a computer and Internet connection can implement quickly and easily.

Step 1: Set Up an Emergency Fund

Protect the Purchasing Power of Your Emergency Cash

In my experience, elegant solutions tend to be relatively simple once you fully understand the problem and come up with an intelligent method to deal with it. That's why this chapter is relatively short, but still important.

As we saw in Chapter 2, if you do nothing about price inflation, then the emergency fund that is designed to cover your expenses for at least 6 months (preferably 12) if you lose your main source of income will steadily lose purchasing power. This will manifest itself by your monthly expenses steadily increasing but the balance in your checking and savings accounts barely changing.

So what can you do to prevent this from being a problem? There are three main solutions, the first of which isn't very practical and doesn't really solve the problem, but I need to mention it because it's what most people choose to do about it.

Increase Your Emergency Fund by the Same Rate That Your Expenses Go Up

The simplest solution to the problem is obvious—if monthly expenses are going up and you want to keep the fund at, say, 12 months worth of expenses, then simply add to the fund each month to make sure the balance is equal to current monthly expenses times 12 at all times.

Figure 3-1 shows exactly how much you'd have to add to your emergency fund each month if your monthly expenses were rising by the 1.18% I mentioned in Chapter 2.

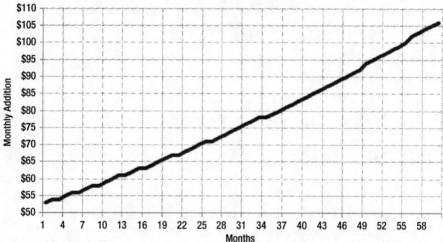

How Much (per month) Mr. & Mrs. Fit Would Have to Add to Their Emergency Fund to Maintain the Purchasing Power if Inflation was 1.18% per Month

Figure 3-1. Maintaining the purchasing power of your emergency fund the hard way

Now this may not seem like a big deal when you initially look at the chart—the monthly addition starts off at a little over $50 and doubles to just over $105 after five years. However, this means that the size of your emergency stash has to *double* just to buy the same amount of products and services it does today. And that's simply to stand still, so to speak, from a quality-of-life point of view.

This is a very inefficient and costly way to maintain your emergency fund, in my opinion, so I'm not recommending you do this.

The Simple Solution: Precious Metals

If you studied the charts in Chapter 2 closely, you'll probably have a good idea what's at the root of the problem. It has to do with the constant weakening of the purchasing power of fiat currencies, such as the dollar, which translates into price increases for physical commodities.

What if, instead of saving cash for your emergency fund, you decided that you would save nonperishable foods from now on? As a result, you stock your cupboard with the equivalent of 12 months' worth of food. If you did that, what period of time would the food in the cupboard feed you for in 1 year, 10 years, or 50 years? The answer is the same of course: it would feed you for 12 months no matter how far into the future you look (assuming you don't change your daily ration significantly). Why? Because it is a physical commodity that doesn't change in size or caloric value *once it's purchased*.

I know the size of products in the stores can shrink, but not normally *after* you've purchased them! Obviously, this solution only works to ensure you will eat during the emergency period. What about other typical monthly expenses like housing, transportation, clothing, entertainment, and other items that can't easily be turned into physical commodities in advance and stored in a cupboard? Yes, I suppose you could purchase all the underwear you'll ever need and put it in a drawer, but what if your taste changes (not to mention your waist size)? Buying all the DVDs you'll ever want to watch in advance is not exactly plausible either unless you only ever want to watch classic movies.

Now you're beginning to see the solution to the emergency fund problem. The fact is that you simply don't want to keep your emergency cash in any fiat currency—you want it in a physical commodity that maintains its purchasing power no matter how long you own it.

You've probably guessed by now. The solution to the problem is to buy precious and industrial metals:

- Gold
- Silver
- Palladium
- Platinum

An Inflation-Proof Emergency Fund That Maintains Purchasing Power

The simplest solution to owning precious metals would be to buy some gold bars and then bury them in the garden (making sure your neighbors don't see you). Take your current monthly expenses, multiply them by 12, divide this number by the current spot price of gold per ounce, and the answer is how many ounces of gold you need to bury in your garden. Then, in ten years, when you lose your job and can't pay your mortgage, simply dig up the bars sell them at the current spot price for dollars, and use the cash to cover your monthly expenses.

If you're looking at the price of gold in US dollars right now and seeing it make new all-time highs, you may be thinking, "Paul, you're nuts. I'm not going to buy into gold right at the high and then watch the value of my emergency cash plummet. The smart money got in months or years ago and is just waiting to cash out at my expense. It's a speculative bubble just waiting to burst."

The only thing I would agree with in that previous paragraph is "the smart money got in months or years ago," but not the part about "waiting to cash out." Take a look at Figure 3-2, which is a chart that shows how many ounces of gold $100,000 would buy over the last decade.

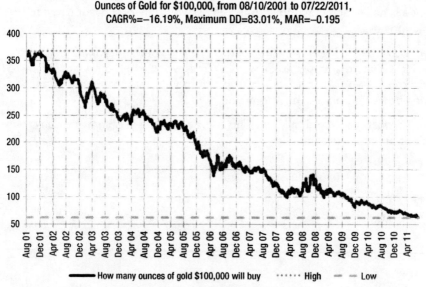

Figure 3-2. Ounces of gold that $100,000 could purchase over the last decade

Does that look like a speculative bubble to you? It looks like a secular trend to me. Another way to look at this is shown in Figure 3-3.

Figure 3-3. Gold priced in Australian dollars, February 1999 to July 2011

It's the same chart shown in Chapter 2 (2-10), but instead it uses Australian dollars instead of US dollars for the "price" of gold. Not such a "speculative bubble" visible there, eh? The fact is that it's not really useful to measure the value of a physical commodity using a fiat paper currency—we should be using the physical commodity to measure the value (or lack thereof) of the fiat paper currency.

If you're really concerned about turning your emergency cash into metals just at an "all-time" high, then simply hedge your bets and average in to your metals positions over a period of time—but be warned, in my opinion this is not the time to be gambling the purchasing power of your emergency fund on the strengthening of the US dollar (or any other fiat currency).

Hopefully you'll now agree that metals are the best place for your emergency fund right now. So let's get back to the practical problems of physical ownership. Following is a list of the immediate ones I could think of:

- What if you can't easily sell your load of gold bars for dollars when you want to?

- What if you've moved to another house and forgotten about the gold bars, and you no longer have access to them?
- What if the US government makes it illegal for individuals to own physical gold in the United States (again)?[1]
- What if you need to make adjustments to the size of the emergency fund because expenses have changed?
- What if you think you can get a job in a couple of months so you don't need to sell a whole gold bar to cover your expenses?
- What if you want to move somewhere else in the world and the US restricts transportation of gold out of the country?
- How practical is this method if you don't want to just own gold, but want platinum or palladium too?

I'm sure there are a few other practical problems you can think of too, and that's why I'm not recommending you own gold bars, gold coins, or gold jewelry. Nor am I recommending you keep gold in your garden, at a security deposit box at a bank, in your own vault at home, or anywhere else actually located inside the United States.

A much better, easier, and more flexible solution to owning metals is using a trustworthy online service. Table 3-1 shows four services that allow you to own precious metals without having to take physical ownership.

Table 3-1. Precious Metal Investment Companies

Company	Jurisdiction	Web Address
Global Gold	Switzerland	globalgold.ch
Perth Mint	Australia	www.perthmint.com.au
Bullion Vault	Great Britain	bullionvault.com
GoldMoney	Channel Islands	www.goldmoney.com

The one I personally use and recommend is GoldMoney.[2]

---

[1] This happened previously in the United States when Executive Order 6102 was signed, on April 5, 1933, by US President Franklin D. Roosevelt. It was repealed on December 31, 1974, by Gerald Ford in Public Law 93-373.

[2] I have no connection to GoldMoney other than as a satisfied customer.

How GoldMoney Works

GoldMoney allows you to deposit cash (currently US dollars, Canadian dollars, British pounds, Swiss francs, Japanese yen, euros, Australian dollars, Hong Kong dollars, or New Zealand dollars) into your account (called a holding). Once it's there, you can purchase metals (currently gold, silver, platinum, and palladium) in small amounts (1/100th of a gram). The metals that you buy are allocated to you and stored on your behalf—for a reasonable monthly fee that is charged in metal, not currency—in one of the vaults that GoldMoney uses. The vaults are located in London, Zurich, and Hong Kong.

You get online access, along with statements of your account holdings and current values, just like a brokerage account. When you want to convert any of your metal holdings back into fiat currency, you simply enter an online order, specify how much of each metal you want to sell, and say which currency you want to receive.

I'm not a tax advisor, and this book is not intended to deal with the tax implications of different investment choices. However, I can give you an overview of the tax treatment of GoldMoney holdings from a US point of view. In the United States, holdings of precious metals would be considered a collectible, and therefore any capital gains from the sale of your Gold-Money holdings would be subject to capital gains taxes. In addition, the capital gains tax for collectibles is 28% in 2011—not the lower 15% for long-term gains in most securities. This, of course, might change, so check with your accountant.

If you move US dollars into your GoldMoney account, purchase metals with them, and leave them alone, then there are no tax implications to deal with until you sell. However, there is an additional reporting requirement for US residents if the value of the account is greater than $10,000. In this case, you must file form TD F 90-22.1 with the US Department of the Treasury before June 30th of the year following the calendar year that the account first had a value of over $10,000. Uncle Sam always wants to know where your assets are, and it's futile trying to hide them. As long as you intend to pay the capital gains taxes due on your holdings when you do sell them, then reporting the account to the US Treasury shouldn't be a problem.

If you do sell some of your metals holdings, then you need to calculate the net capital gain (minus the fees that have been charged for the storage of your holdings during the period) and report this on your tax return as a capital gain. GoldMoney does not issue 1099 forms to US-resident customers, but your complete transaction history is available as part of the online access to your account, so it should not be a problem for you, or your tax advisor, to calculate the capital gains just like for any other investments you sell.

The following narrative describes how The Fits implement their emergency fund.

Mr. & Mrs. Fit Establish an Emergency Fund

Mr. and Mrs. Fit decide to open a GoldMoney account and use it to manage their emergency fund cash. Mr. Fit goes to GoldMoney.com and downloads the application form. He prints it out, fills it in, and mails it along with the supporting identification documentation. Once he receives notification that the account is open, he moves all their current US dollars into his checking account and writes a check to fund his GoldMoney account for $60,000.

When the check has cleared, his GoldMoney account access shows a balance of $60,000. Mr. Fit then uses this cash to buy equal dollar amounts of gold, silver, palladium, and platinum for their account. He receives the following holdings:

Metal	Ounces
Gold	8.0196
Silver	289.7581
Palladium	6.5372
Platinum	15.1961

Now that he's done that, Mr. Fit doesn't need to worry about his emergency fund any longer. Even though the dollar value of his account will fluctuate daily, he knows that over the long-term, when he needs to convert his holdings back to currency, he will have the same purchasing power that he has now. He only needs to make an adjustment if his monthly expenses increase significantly (due to adding liabilities, not price inflation). In this case, he will add to his metals holdings by moving more cash into his GoldMoney account and purchasing equal dollar amounts of additional metals.

For example, if he adds a significant monthly expense of $1,000 per month, he would add $12,000 to his GoldMoney account and purchase $3,000 worth of each metal at the current spot price.

Gold vs. the Dollar

At this point you may be saying, "That's all fine, but what if the value of the US dollar significantly strengthens vs. gold? Won't I end up with a shortfall in my emergency fund if I need it?" The simple answer is that this is very unlikely to happen, and if it does, then it's not going to be a problem anyway. If the US dollar is strengthening, inflation is very low, the economy is growing, unemployment is low, the government is doing a great job of managing fiscal policy, then everyone's standard of living will be going up. So you shouldn't be needing your emergency fund any time soon, should you?

If you aren't participating in the financial nirvana for some reason and you need to tap your emergency fund when the value of your precious metals holdings are relatively low (when measured in dollars), remember that you don't have to sell your entire metals holding as soon as you lose your main source of income. If you set up your fund with 12 months' worth of cash, then you can sell 1/12 of your metal positions each month to cover expenses until you replace the income you have lost. This should smooth out any volatility in the value of your emergency fund over a longer period of time. In addition, your emergency fund should not be the only place for you to "park" excess assets – you should have savings that are designed to increase in value if and when fiat currencies are worth holding and use these cash resources if the value of your emergency fund is temporarily depressed.

Chapter 4 explains how to manage your working capital and savings in this kind of utopian environment (and the normal kind too), and Chapter 5 explains how to make a good risk-adjusted return on your investments regardless what's going on with inflation, interest rates, and global currencies. These three steps together help you manage your finances and preserve your wealth regardless of the prevailing economic conditions.

An Alternative Solution, for People with Home Equity to Spare

Earlier in this chapter I mentioned that there were three solutions to the emergency fund problem. We've dealt with two of them (adding to the fund monthly and using precious metals), and now it's time to explain the third one.

Wouldn't it be great if you could have an emergency fund that had the following characteristics?

- It didn't cost you anything until you needed to use it.
- It could be increased and decreased as expenses changed.
- It was cheap to set up.
- It didn't require a large cash deposit at the start.

Fortunately, if you have spare equity in your home (i.e., the current market value of your home is greater than the outstanding balance on your mortgage), then you can use a home equity line of credit (HELOC) as your emergency fund instead of cash in your checking account.

A word of caution here. The old saying that a bank is an institution that lends money only to people who don't need it is true. A HELOC, just like a mortgage, is a loan *against future income* that is secured on a property so you get a better rate than for an unsecured loan. This means that if you don't have any income, you won't be approved for a HELOC no matter how much equity you have in your home based on its current value. Therefore, this technique should be put in place in advance, before you lose your primary income—not afterward. So if this idea appeals to you, make a call *now* to your friendly banker.

Inflation will still continue to eat away at the spending power of your HELOC (although this won't cost you anything since it's simply a line of credit you haven't used yet), so it's a good idea to take advantage of any significant local increases in house prices. Get your home revalued, and if it has gone up, then apply for an increase in the HELOC amount too. This way your line of credit can keep up with inflation as long as house prices don't go down the toilet. This is the main reason why using a HELOC should be a secondary method of implementing an emergency fund—it's still a good idea to have some funds in precious metals as well.

Another caution is that if you're the kind of person who will be tempted to use "just a little" of the HELOC for that "emergency" vacation in Hawaii you've always wanted to take, then this technique is probably not for you. Use precious metals instead.

If you currently have cash sitting in a checking account as your emergency fund, but also have a mortgage on your house, then simply use the cash to pay down the mortgage principal and put a line of credit in place that is the same size as the cash you paid off the mortgage. This is usually simpler if you take out the HELOC with the same company that is giving you the primary mortgage on your home. So it's best to wait until next time you want to refinance your primary mortgage and then talk to the bank about the line of credit at the same time. Again, don't wait until after you lose your primary income to do any of this—the bank won't approve any type of loan if you don't have any current income.

If you end up in the situation where you are forced to use your HELOC to pay monthly expenses, it's not all bad. In an inflationary environment where prices are going up, it's better to be a debtor than a creditor—you can pay back borrowed funds with devalued currency units since the balance doesn't grow and the value of the currency units you use to pay the interest on the loan is constantly shrinking. Once you replace your primary income you can simply start to pay down the HELOC until it's down to zero again.

In Summary

This chapter has outlined two practical solutions to implement an emergency fund that should maintain purchasing power over time.

These solutions are:

- Using GoldMoney to own and manage precious metals online
- Utilizing a HELOC if you have (or can create) equity in your home

If you follow one or both of these solutions, you will no longer have to worry about the purchasing power of your emergency fund being significantly diminished when you need it. Although the value as measured by any one currency will be volatile, the purchasing power of the physical metals that you hold should be much more stable and resilient to the ravages of inflation.

Step 2: Make Savings and Working Capital Work for You

How to Maintain an Acceptable Real Rate of Return in Different Interest Rate Environments

So far, we've seen how to protect the purchasing power of your emergency fund so that it will have an excellent chance of paying your fixed expenses when you need it. The solution to the problem of inflation works well for funds that need to maintain purchasing power, but it has a drawback if you need to guarantee the dollar value of a certain portion of your cash assets in the near future. The dollar value of metals in your online precious metals account can go up as well as down in the short term, because the price is volatile.

For cash that you are going to need to meet specific obligations in the near term (like college expenses, a vacation you're saving up for, a major purchase like a new vehicle, or the deposit on a new house), you have a different set of requirements. If this is cash that you simply can't afford to take any risk with at all—like next semester's college tuition payment—then there is no alternative but to keep it in cash and accept the negative real rate of return. Remember that risk and reward always go hand in hand, so if you need to take zero risk, then you cannot expect any reward. Any method of capital management that generates a return involves risk (in the form of price volatility) and therefore should not be used for cash that needs to maintain its near-term dollar value.

The method that I describe in the rest of this chapter is for cash that you *can* afford to take some risk with in order to have a reasonable chance of a decent real rate of return. How to deal with your savings and working capital depends on what the prevailing interest rate environment is for all major currencies.

It would be great if a major currency always paid an annual interest rate a few percentage points above the inflation rate. If your home currency always did this, then you would not have any problems at all. Unfortunately, there are many periods (about 80% of the time, as you'll see before the end of this chapter) where this is not the case. So there is no simple, single-currency solution to this negative real interest rate problem.

Did I say *currency?* Yes. Holding foreign currency can be an important way to hedge against inflation. And it need not cause undue stress—buying currency is not much different, you'll see, than buying stocks or bonds.

First, I need to define what *real rate of return* means. The real rate of return on an investment is simply the actual (or nominal) rate of return you have received, minus the current rate of inflation. So if you buy a certificate of deposit (CD) in US dollars that pays 6% per year in interest, and the current CPI-U inflation rate is 2%, then the real rate of return is 6% – 2% = 4%. For the purposes of this chapter, we're going to ignore the caveats of the CPI calculations discussed in Chapter 2, and assume that the CPI-U does represent a "fair" inflation rate with regard to the purchasing power of your cash.

When deciding what to do with savings or working capital, the first thing we need to do is define whether we're in a positive or negative real interest rate environment. For this we need to know two things:

- The current annual interest rate payable in each major currency listed below

- The current annual inflation rate for each home country or geographic area for the currency

The ten major currencies I consider when doing this calculation are

- Australian dollar
- British pound
- Canadian dollar
- Euro
- Hong Kong dollar
- Japanese yen
- New Zealand dollar
- Swedish krona
- Swiss franc
- US dollar

Table 4-1 shows the current interest rates, inflation rates, and real rate of return for each of the ten currencies, as of April 2011.[1]

Table 4-1. Real Rate of Return on Ten Major Currencies, April 2011

Currency	Currency Symbol	Benchmark Rate	Brokerage Fee	Interest Paid	Inflation Rate	Real Rate
Australian dollar	AUD	4.761%	0.500%	4.261%	2.700%	1.561%
British pound	GBP	0.572%	0.500%	0.072%	4.000%	−3.928%
Canadian dollar	CAD	0.965%	0.500%	0.465%	3.300%	−2.835%
Euro	EUR	1.434%	0.500%	0.934%	2.700%	−1.766%
Hong Kong dollar	HKD	0.050%	0.750%	0.000%	4.600%	−4.600%
Japanese yen	JPY	0.116%	0.500%	0.000%	0.000%	0.000%
New Zealand dollar	NZD	2.500%	2.500%	0.000%	4.500%	−4.500%
Swedish krona	SEK	1.828%	0.500%	1.328%	2.900%	−1.572%
Swiss franc	CHF	0.068%	0.500%	0.000%	1.000%	−1.000%
US dollar	USD	0.100%	0.500%	0.000%	2.700%	−2.700%

---

[1] The resources that were used to determine the data are listed in Appendix A.

As you can see, as of April 2011, only the Australian dollar is paying a positive real rate of interest. This means if you have any cash in any of the other nine major currencies, then the purchasing power of that cash is diminishing every single day. Note that it's important to include any fee or spread that your broker or bank charges, or any other deductions from the actual interest you will receive on each currency balance. If the current benchmark rate is less than the interest fee, then the interest paid will be zero, not negative (i.e., you will not normally be charged for holding positive currency balances in your account).

Once you have constructed this table, then it's easy to determine whether you are in a positive or negative real interest rate environment and act accordingly. If at least eight out of ten of the major currencies are paying a real rate of interest that is at least 2% per annum, then you are in a *positive real interest rate environment*; otherwise, you're in a *zero or negative real interest rate environment*.

A Positive Real Interest Rate Environment: What to Do

If you're in a positive real interest rate environment, then it's a good idea to keep savings and working capital in major currencies. The best approach is to hold currencies proportional to their real interest rate. The following example should make this clear. Let's assume that prevailing interest rates for at least eight of the ten currencies are at least 2% above inflation, as in Table 4-2.

Table 4-2. Rate of Return on Ten Major Currencies in a Fictitious Positive Real Interest Rate Environment

Currency	Currency Symbol	Benchmark Rate	Interest Fee	Interest Paid	Inflation Rate	Real Rate
Australian dollar	AUD	7.761%	0.500%	7.261%	2.700%	4.561%
British pound	GBP	6.572%	0.500%	6.072%	4.000%	2.072%
Canadian dollar	CAD	4.965%	0.500%	4.465%	3.300%	1.165%
Euro	EUR	6.434%	0.500%	5.934%	2.700%	3.234%
Hong Kong dollar	HKD	9.050%	0.750%	8.300%	4.600%	3.700%
Japanese yen	JPY	5.116%	0.500%	4.616%	0.000%	4.616%

Currency	Currency Symbol	Benchmark Rate	Interest Fee	Interest Paid	Inflation Rate	Real Rate
New Zealand dollar	NZD	9.500%	2.500%	7.000%	4.500%	2.500%
Swedish krona	SEK	8.828%	0.500%	8.328%	2.900%	5.428%
Swiss franc	CHF	4.068%	0.500%	3.568%	1.000%	2.568%
US dollar	USD	6.100%	0.500%	5.600%	2.700%	2.900%

To determine how much of your capital to allocate to each currency, we simply need to construct another table that determines the relative weighting of each currency based on its real interest rate. This is shown in Table 4-3.

Table 4-3. Currency Weighting for the Purpose of Allocating Capital

Currency	Currency Symbol	Real Rate	Currency Weighting
Australian dollar	AUD	4.561%	14%
British pound	GBP	2.072%	6%
Canadian dollar	CAD	1.165%	4%
Euro	EUR	3.234%	10%
Hong Kong dollar	HKD	3.700%	11%
Japanese yen	JPY	4.616%	14%
New Zealand dollar	NZD	2.500%	8%
Swedish krona	SEK	5.428%	17%
Swiss franc	CHF	2.568%	8%
US dollar	USD	2.900%	9%
	Total	32.744%	100%

How did I come up with these figures? The currency weightings are simply each individual real rate divided by the total of the real rates (32.744% in this example). For example, Australia's 4.561% rate of return divided by 32.744 results in 14% (rounded). Once you have constructed the table, then it's simple to work out how much of each currency you should buy. If you have $100,000, for example, then according to Table 4-3 you should put 6% of it, or $6,000, into British pounds. If the current exchange rate between

US dollars and British pounds is 1.6489 (i.e., 1 British pound is worth 1.6489 US dollars), then you would buy 6,000 / 1.6489 = 3,638 GBP.

Table 4-4 shows how you would allocate $100,000 US dollars based on the given exchange rates.

Table 4-4. Allocation of $100,000 into Ten Major Currencies

Currency	Currency Symbol	Real Rate	Currency Weighting	Exchange Rate	Dollar Allocation	Currency Allocation
Australian dollar	AUD	4.561%	14%	1.0778	13,929	12,924
British pound	GBP	2.072%	6%	1.6489	6,328	3,838
Canadian dollar	CAD	1.165%	4%	1.0491	3,558	3,391
Euro	EUR	3.234%	10%	1.4635	9,877	6,749
Hong Kong dollar	HKD	3.700%	11%	0.1287	11,300	87,801
Japanese yen	JPY	4.616%	14%	0.0122	14,097	1,155,492
New Zealand dollar	NZD	2.500%	8%	0.8052	7,635	9,482
Swedish krona	SEK	5.428%	17%	0.1637	16,577	101,265
Swiss franc	CHF	2.568%	8%	1.1397	7,843	6,882
US dollar	USD	2.900%	9%	1.0000	8,856	8,856
Total		32.744%	100%		$100,000	

Using the details from Table 4-4, you would take your 100,000 US dollars and buy 1,155,492 Japanese yen with 14% of the US dollars you have. Once you have purchased all the correct amounts of all the currencies with your US dollars, the balances in your account would look like Table 4-5.

Table 4-5. Currency Holdings After Purchase

Currency	Currency Symbol	Currency Balance
Australian dollar	AUD	12,922
British pound	GBP	3,838
Canadian dollar	CAD	3,391
Euro	EUR	6,750

Currency	Currency Symbol	Currency Balance
Hong Kong dollar	HKD	87,801
Japanese yen	JPY	1,155,492
New Zealand dollar	NZD	9,482
Swedish krona	SEK	101,265
Swiss franc	CHF	6,882
US dollar	USD	8,856

So, instead of having 100,000 US dollars, you would only have 8,856 US dollars remaining, and the rest would be held in the other nine currencies.

There are a couple of choices when it comes to which firm to use to implement the cash rebalancing method. These are:

- Everbank
- Interactive Brokers

The simplest way to implement this approach would be to use an Interactive Brokers (IB) account. The advantage of using IB is that the firm offers multicurrency accounts by default. Interest accrues daily in all currency balances, and you can easily switch between all the major currencies in one account with low fees for the transactions. The "base" currency of the account is basically just a reporting currency (which may be switched at any time), and the only practical implication of the base currency for the account is that it is the currency that commissions on foreign exchange (FX) trades are charged in.

Another advantage of using IB is that the universal account is an online brokerage account too, so you can use it for the second part of the cash rebalancing method (described in the next section), and also to manage your investments, as described in Chapter 5.

IB is not a full-service, hand-holding type of brokerage. It is fully electronic with online access, and it expects its customers to know what they are doing. If you find this intimidating, then it's probably best to break up the process into several simple steps:

1. Open an individual universal account by going to IB's website, www.interactivebrokers.com, and filling out the application online for an account that allows you to trade equities and FX.

2. Send the required identification information that is requested once the account application is completed.

3. Once the account is approved, fund it by writing a check or wiring funds *with the minimum required amount.*

4. Log onto the demonstration version of the account and familiarize yourself with how to place currency transactions accurately.

5. Build a spreadsheet to allow you to manage the currency balances effectively in the demo account until you are comfortable with the process.

6. Manage the currency balances in your real account using the Web-Trader application, which is simpler to use than the full Trader Workstation (TWS) application.

7. Only when you are completely comfortable with the whole process should you increase the funding of the IB account to include all the savings and working capital you want to apply to this method.

PECULIARITIES OF CURRENCY TRADING

When trading currencies, there are a few things to watch out for. Firstly, it's important to note that there are always two currencies involved in a FX trade. These are called the base currency and the quote currency. For example, in the FX pair GBP/USD (or GBP.USD), GBP is the base and USD is the quote. If the "price" of the FX pair GBP/USD is quoted as 1.6, for example, this means that 1 GBP will buy 1.6 USD.

Traditionally, some pairs are always quoted with US dollars as the base currency. These are

- USD/CAD

- USD/CHF

- USD/HKD

- USD/JPY

- USD/SEK

When you want to do FX trades in these quote currencies, you will have to sell the desired quantity of US dollars in order to buy the quote currencies (just as you would expect).

The other currencies you may want to trade are traditionally listed as the base currency with US dollars being the quote currency. They are as follows:

- AUD/USD
- EUR/USD
- GBP/USD
- NZD/USD

When you want to do FX trades in these base currencies, you simply have to buy the currency pair, which in turn means you are selling US dollars to purchase the base currency. This means that you will have to calculate the amount of base currency you wish to buy, rather than the quantity of US dollars you wish to sell, as in the first group of currencies where the base currency is US dollars.

If you're thinking that this all sounds a bit too complicated, or you don't want to open up yet another brokerage account, then there is a simpler alternative to actually doing the FX transactions; you can use currency exchange-traded funds (ETFs) instead.

The following table shows you possible choices for each of the major currencies.

Currency	Currency Symbol	Rydex ETF Symbol	Dreyfus ETF Symbol
Australian dollar	AUD	FXA	-
British pound	GBP	FXB	-
Canadian dollar	CAD	FXC	-
Euro	EUR	FXE	EU
Hong Kong dollar	HKD	-	-
Japanese yen	JPY	FXY	JYF
New Zealand dollar	NZD	-	BNZ
Swedish krona	SEK	FXS	-
Swiss franc	CHF	FXF	-
US dollar	USD	-	-

The two firms currently offering currency ETFs are Rydex (CurrencyShares) and Dreyfus (WisdomTree). There is not currently a Hong Kong dollar ETF available, so that particular currency would have to be omitted from the method if you chose to implement it using ETFs.

One caveat with the Rydex funds is that they are mainly designed to track the exchange rate rather than both the exchange rate and the interest payable. After the fees charged by the fund and the spread charged by the firm providing the depository account are deducted, there is no guarantee that you will actually receive a reasonable annual rate of interest based on the relevant currency benchmark rate. For this reason I would recommend the Dreyfus WisdomTree ETFs where available (EUR, JPY, and NZD) and the Rydex CurrencyShares ETFs for the remainder. Note that, as with everything in investing, opting for simplicity has a cost, and can have a significant detrimental effect on performance. There is no guarantee that you will be able to achieve results similar to actually using real currency transactions with daily accrued interest in an IB account.

Once you have managed to accurately establish currency balances in proportion to the interest rates with a fully funded account, then quarterly rebalancing should be sufficient unless there is significant change in real interest rates or currency exchange rates. Unless a particular currency is more than 5% out of balance, it's best to leave things unchanged—this minimizes commissions and fees on the account and therefore maximizes your return overall. The easiest way to track this is in a spreadsheet with all the required information in it, as in Table 4-6.

Table 4-6. Spreadsheet Showing Ideal and Actual Allocations of a FX Account

Currency	Currency Symbol	Current Balance	Required Balance	Percent Difference
Australian dollar	AUD	12,922	13,439	4%
British pound	GBP	3,838	4,068	6%
Canadian dollar	CAD	3,391	3,289	–3%
Euro	EUR	6,750	6,885	2%
Hong Kong dollar	HKD	87,801	88,679	1%
Japanese yen	JPY	1,155,492	1,178,602	2%
New Zealand dollar	NZD	9,482	8,534	–10%
Swedish krona	SEK	101,265	102,278	1%
Swiss franc	CHF	6,883	6,952	1%
US dollar	USD	8,856	8,856	0%

What you need to do is to update the interest rates, CPI numbers, and exchange rates, and then recalculate the currency balances on a quarterly basis and make any modifications necessary to get the balance back (to within 5%) if something changes. For example, in Table 4-6, the British pound and New Zealand dollar balances are now out of balance by more than 5% (positive or negative), so we need to sell some New Zealand dollars and buy British pounds with them to get the balances back in line.

If the current exchange rate between British pounds and New Zealand dollars is 2.047 (i.e., 1 British pound purchases 2.047 New Zealand dollars), then we could sell 9482 − 8534 = 948 NZD and receive 948 / 2.047 = 463 GBP for them. The currency balances would then look like Table 4-7.

Table 4-7. FX Account After Rebalancing

Currency	Currency Symbol	Current Balance	Required Balance	Percent Difference
Australian dollar	AUD	12,922	13,439	4%
British pound	GBP	4,301	4,068	−5%
Canadian dollar	CAD	3,391	3,289	−3%
Euro	EUR	6,750	6,885	2%
Hong Kong dollar	HKD	87,801	88,679	1%
Japanese yen	JPY	1,155,492	1,178,602	2%
New Zealand dollar	NZD	8,534	8,534	0%
Swedish krona	SEK	101,265	102,278	1%
Swiss franc	CHF	6,883	6,952	1%
US dollar	USD	8,856	8,856	0%

Selling the currencies that are overweighted and buying the currencies that are underweighted with them allows us to keep the balances within the 5% tolerance. This should be done on a quarterly basis, with the minimum number of transactions, in order to minimize the fees required to implement the method.

A Low or Negative Real Interest Rate Environment: What to Do

If we're currently in a low or negative real interest rate environment, then keeping savings in major currencies does not make sense—the purchasing power is being diminished every single day. In this kind of environment it's best to allocate equally to metals, ETFs, inflation-protected ETFs, and inverse bond ETFs. (Inverse bond funds are designed to move in the opposite direction of the ETF they are paired with—more on those to come.) The selection I recommend is

- Gold (GLD)
- Silver (SLV)
- Platinum (PPLT)
- Palladium (PALL)
- Inverse Treasury Bonds (TBT)
- Treasury Inflation Protected Securities (TIP)

If your home currency is paying a positive real interest rate, then you can include an allocation to that, as well as the ETFs listed.

Please note that buying an inverse fund like TBT is not the same as shorting a security. Selling short cannot be done in a retirement account because it requires trading on margin—and retirement accounts can only be cash accounts. Therefore, to ensure this method can be implemented in any brokerage or retirement account, it's better to use inverse funds. In this instance, TBT is a security that is bought, but the fund is designed to move in the opposite direction of another fund—in this case to TLT, which is the iShares Trust Barclays 20+ Year Treasury Bond Fund. Figure 4-1 shows a chart of TBT and TLT over the last three years.

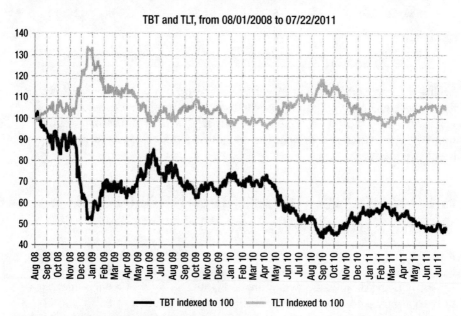

Figure 4-1. TBT and TLT over the last three years

Note that TBT is designed to move twice as much in the opposite direction as any move in TLT, so a 2% move up in TLT should correspond to a 4% move down in TBT. You may be looking at Figure 4-1 and thinking, "Paul, you must be nuts. Why would I want to put cash into something that has lost about 50% of its value in only three years?" The one thing I need to make clear here is that hindsight is always 20:20—interest rates have stayed very low for this whole period and therefore bond prices (which move opposite to interest rates) have stayed high, so TLT has gone up and sideways while TBT has gone down (twice as much) and sideways.

The reason TBT is included in this portfolio is so it does the following:

- Diversifies from simply holding metals ETFs
- Will make a good return for periods in which interest rates are rising but inflation is also rising, such that currencies are not paying a real rate of return yet

The second point here simply has not happened (yet), so the TBT part of the portfolio will be losing money right now. In the testing I performed for this method, going back way before TBT existed, I created a synthetic TBT that moved inversely to yields on US treasuries and included it in the portfolio. It increased CAGR and decreased DD overall, so it's definitely worth including.

The same goes for including TIP, even though we know that the CPI-U understates real inflation. The extra diversification provided by including TIP is worth the caveats and problems. Again, my historical testing shows this to be the case.

Table 4-8 shows what the allocation would be as of April 2011 for the same $100,000 in cash we dealt with in the previous section (concerning a positive real interest rate environment). Since US dollars are not paying a positive real rate of interest, the $100,000 will be equally allocated to the six ETFs. If US dollars were included, then the allocation would be one-seventh to each ETF and one-seventh to US dollars.

Table 4-8. Allocation of $100,000 in a Mixed Portfolio of Metals, Commodities, and Currency

ETF or Home Currency	Currency Symbol	Current Price	Shares Allocated	US Dollar Value
Gold	GLD	149.88	111	$16,637
Silver	SLV	40.58	410	$16,638
Palladium	PALL	76.89	216	$16,608

ETF or Home Currency	Currency Symbol	Current Price	Shares Allocated	US Dollar Value
Platinum	PPLT	183.94	90	$16,555
Inverse bonds	TBT	35.09	474	$16,633
Treasury Inflation Protected	TIP	110.93	150	$16,640
US dollar	USD	1.00	0	0
			Total	$99,709

The total is slightly less than $100,000 since we have to round down the number of shares purchased to the nearest whole share. The allocations if US dollars were also included are shown in Table 4-9.

Table 4-9. Allocation of $100,000 in a Mixed Portfolio That Includes US Dollars

ETF or Home Currency	Currency Symbol	Current Price	Shares Allocated	US Dollar Value
Gold	GLD	149.88	95	$14,239
Silver	SLV	40.58	352	$14,284
Palladium	PALL	76.89	185	$14,225
Platinum	PPLT	183.94	77	$14,163
Inverse bonds	TBT	35.09	407	$14,282
Treasury Inflation Protected	TIP	110.93	128	$14,199
US dollar	USD	1.00	14609	$14,609
			Total	$100,000

The reason it's a good idea to include an inverse bond fund is that if interest rates are very low, then they only really have one way to go: up. And since bond prices move opposite to interest rates, when rates inevitably go up, then bond prices will go down (and you'll make money being long an inverse bond fund). Also, if inflation does increase significantly, then TIP will go up as well, even if it's not as much as real inflation "in the street."

If you want further diversification, you could add commodity ETFs such as the following:

- Coffee (JO)
- Agribusiness (MOO)
- Natural gas (UNG)
- US oil (USO)

If you're thinking that these commodities are all susceptible to speculative bubbles and manipulation by industry participants and professional traders, and you don't want to compete with these people, then simply construct a chart of each commodity priced in ounces of gold rather than US dollars and see where the "speculative bubbles" are then. Remember the chart of oil priced in gold from Chapter 2? Once the effects of currency exchange rate movements and devaluation are removed from the chart, it generally shows a much more stable mean-reverting relationship for each commodity.

However, these ETFs are more likely to be included in your investment account management, which is covered in Chapter 5. This chapter is specifically about savings and working capital, not investment accounts. If you plan to include commodity ETFs in your investment account, then they should not be included in the rebalancing ETFs you use for your savings. You don't want to end up with an overallocation to these particular ETFs.

If you have opened an IB account, then all these ETFs will be automatically available for you to trade in this account, and the switch from currencies to ETFs should be relatively simple.

Historical Results

As with everything in trading and investing, it's best to test the implications of any decisions you make about how to manage your investments. I have spent many years researching different investment management techniques, and the method of cash rebalancing described in this chapter is the most effective method I have found. It minimizes volatility, minimizes exposure to a single currency, and generates a positive real rate of return. Test results for the last 16 years are shown in Figure 4-2.

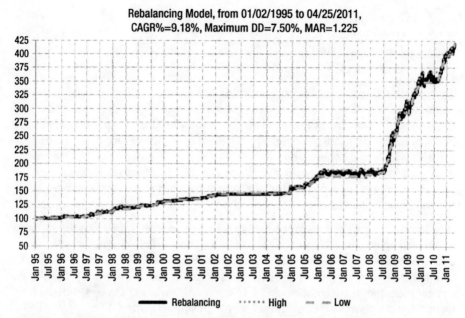

Figure 4-2. Rebalancing model, 1/2/1995 to 4/25/2011, indexed to 100

These results were generated by a product called Trading Blox, which is a sophisticated historical testing environment. Note that these results do not take historical inflation rates into account—only benchmark rates minus the fees charged by IB. Thus, it is not an exact simulation of the method described here.

These results are only meant to be an indication of the kind of return and volatility this type of method generates—not an accurate estimation of future returns using the exact method described in this chapter. Note that as the CAGR has increased over the last three years, so has the maximum DD, but it has still remained under control and produced a reasonable *risk-adjusted return* without excessive volatility for the period.

Note that some of the ETFs in the test sample did not exist for the whole period, and have been replaced by a similar proxy instrument. For example, SLV has been replaced by silver futures data for periods before it existed as an ETF.

Figure 4-3 shows how the method switched from currency rebalancing to ETF rebalancing over the test period.

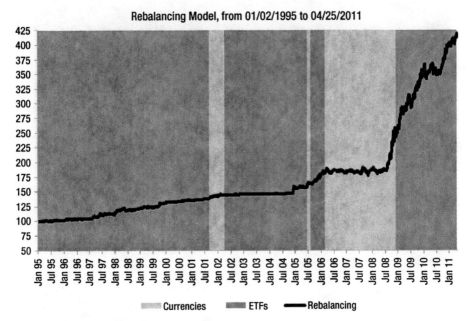

Figure 4-3. Rebalancing model showing switching between currencies and ETFs

Over the 16-year test, there were three periods where currency rebalancing was used, and four periods where ETF rebalancing was used. Overall, currency rebalancing was only used about 20% of the time and ETFs 80% of the time.

In Summary

Effectively managing your savings and working capital depends on what the prevailing interest rate environment is. If it's a low or negative real interest rate environment, then keep your capital in metals ETFs and inverse bond funds. If it's a positive real interest rate environment, then keep your savings in major currencies proportional to the real interest rate they are paying.

In this way you will maximize the rate of return on your savings and minimize the volatility of the absolute value of your savings accounts at the same time. This cash rebalancing technique should also be used for any "spare capital" that is not currently being utilized to take risk in your investment accounts. How to actually make a good risk-adjusted return in your investments accounts will be covered in the next chapter.

Step 3: Generate a Good Risk-Adjusted Return on Investments

How to Successfully Manage Your Own Investment Accounts

This chapter is all about effectively managing your investment accounts. If you're like most people I talk to, you have at least one brokerage account, possibly a 401(k) with your current (or a previous) employer, and maybe even an Individual Retirement Account (IRA) as well.

In the 401(k), you will probably be contributing a fixed percentage of your salary each month, your employer will be doing matching contributions, and then the whole lot will be fully invested using the "percentage allocation" model you set when you joined the company and then forgot about.

In your IRA, you're probably buying and holding (aka buying and hoping), dollar cost averaging, or putting it all into a fund that automatically adjusts your equity/bond/cash balance over time. If you're a sophisticated investor, you might even be choosing a diversified portfolio of investments yourself and doing some sort of periodic rebalancing.

In your brokerage account you're probably doing some combination of the above, along with a little bit of whatever you just heard on CNBC, whatever you just read in the *Wall Street Journal*, whatever your brother-in-law just invested in, and any other random investment methods and ideas that you made up as you went along or were recommended to you by someone in the financial industry.

Before we even get to thinking about how to effectively manage any investment account (retirement or otherwise), it's important that you grasp three major concepts. You need to:

- Know exactly how to determine your current risk-adjusted return for each account and understand whether this is acceptable or not
- Understand what a complete investment method looks like
- Know how to construct a complete investment method that can be operated in your account, and also have the dedication, skill, and knowledge required to accurately implement it

This may sound scary, but it's relatively straightforward. And you don't need to quit your day job to find the time you need to accomplish your goals. Far from it. But you do need to be committed to taking control of your finances.

Let's cover how to measure and interpret your risk-adjusted return first, since this will tell you whether you're an investment genius or whether you're taking way to much risk for far too little return in your investment accounts. My money is on the latter, by the way.

How to Measure Risk-Adjusted Return Effectively

Measuring the performance of your investment account is not a complicated affair, but it is essential that you understand how to do it in a representative way. Just because your account balance is going up (especially if you're making contributions to it along the way) doesn't mean you're generating good results. Remember Figure 2-8 in Chapter 2 that showed what dollar cost averaging in SPY (the S&P 500 ETF) looked like over the last ten years? The chart was sloping in the right direction (upward), but the return being achieved in the context of the risk being taken was just terrible.

So, how do we measure risk and return effectively?

Let's Look at Return

Most people can easily grasp the concept of return. Do I have more or less than I started off with? If the answer is, "Yes, I have more," then it's a pretty simple calculation to turn this into a percentage. For example, if you start with $100,000 and your account now has a value of $120,000, then you have a 20% return:

$$(\$120{,}000 - \$100{,}000) / \$100{,}000 = 20\%$$

Is that a good result? That depends on two things; one is simple to determine, and one is a little harder and is nearly always ignored by most people. The first is *how long it took to generate the return.* If you made 20% in one year, then that's pretty good. If you made 20% in ten years, then that's not so great. In order to take time into account, it's essential to calculate the compound annual growth rate (CAGR), rather than simply the total percentage return.

The CAGR is the annual rate of return that gives you the total return achieved (20% in our example) over the time period being measured. In our example, if it took one year, then the calculation is simple—you made 20% in one year. Therefore, the CAGR is equal to 20%.

In the example where it took ten years, we need to determine how much per year (as a percentage) you would have to make for the total return to equal 20% after ten years. This is easy to do in a spreadsheet by using the POWER function. If you know the total return percentage as a decimal (Total Return in the following equation), and the number of years, then you can use the following formula to determine the CAGR percentage:

$$CAGR = POWER\ (1 + Total\ Return\ ,\ 1\ /\ Number\ of\ Years) - 1$$

In this example, where Total Return is 0.20 and the number of years is 10, we have the following:

$$CAGR = POWER\ (1.2,\ 1\ /\ 10) - 1$$

This gives an answer of 1.84% (rounded), meaning that the CAGR is 1.84% if you made 20% in total over ten years. You can check this answer by reversing the formula. If you know the CAGR as a decimal CAGR, and the number of years, then you can work out the total return by using the following formula:

Total Return = POWER (1 + CAGR, Number of Years) – 1

which in this case is:

Total Return = POWER (1.0184, 10) – 1

This gives the answer 20%, meaning that 1.84% compounded for ten years turns into 20%. Note that in our example we started off with a fixed amount of $100,000, which grew to $120,000 over the period. If you had made additional contributions during that time, then it's important to deduct them from the return made before attempting to calculate the CAGR.

But if you really want to include all your contributions, it can be done. There are lots of complicated ways of determining actual return when there have been contributions and withdrawals from an account, but for our purposes we can use the following simple formula:

(Ending Value – Total Investment) / Total Investment

So, in our example, if you had started with $100,000 and added $5000 in total over ten years, and the ending value was still $120,000, then the total return was

($120,000 – $100,000 – $5,000) / ($100,000 + $5,000)

This gives us 14.29% for our total return, and using the POWER function formula from before, a CAGR of 1.4%.

Let's Look at Risk

So now that we've taken care of the return side of the problem by determining the CAGR, we need to look at the second thing I mentioned: the risk side of the problem.

If I told you I knew of a method that would provide a CAGR of 50%, you would probably think that sounded great. If you had $100,000 to invest, in ten years time that would be worth $5,766,504 if you just left it alone to compound! You may be thinking, "Where do I send the check?"

Naturally, there's a catch. During that time period, you would have had to suffer over a 90% loss. At some point your account could have been worth only $10,000. Does it sound like a good idea now? Could your nerves handle it? This is the key point—CAGR is only meaningful if you know the risk (as represented by the maximum loss that was incurred during the period) that was taken to achieve it. This is where maximum drawdown (DD) comes in.

Calculating a percentage DD is a little trickier than calculating the CAGR. What you need to do is establish the periodic value of your account and then plug these numbers into a spreadsheet. If this is an account where you have simply invested an initial amount of cash and then bought and sold securities in it, then a simple monthly total value will suffice for the life of the account.

If you have made repeating or periodic contributions to (or withdrawals from) the account, then the calculation is a little more complex. Each monthly total value must be modified to deduct each previous additional contribution (or add back each previous withdrawal) so you can calculate the CAGR on your investments not including withdrawals and contributions.

Then you can calculate the highest highs and the subsequent lowest lows, and work out the maximum percentage decline from a high (peak) to a low (trough). Once you have done this, then you have the two components of the MAR ratio:

$$\text{MAR Ratio} = \text{CAGR \% / Maximum Drawdown \%}$$

Using the MAR ratio, we can directly compare any investment techniques to see if they are providing a reasonable risk-adjusted return. Note that a MAR ratio of 1.0 is impossible to maintain over long periods of time. The CAGR is being earned every year, but the DD is tolerated only once and recovered from. A MAR ratio of 0.5 is a more achievable target, and this is still vastly superior to "traditional" investment account methods that provide little (or negative) return coupled with large, uncontrolled drawdowns.

A good homework exercise right now would be to do some number crunching to calculate the MAR ratio of all your investment accounts over the last ten years. This should be done on a "total account" basis, rather than on individual positions. It would be even better if you could aggregate all your accounts together into one master account that represents all your investing activity.

I'm sure the numbers will be both interesting and eye-opening, especially if you have never done any kind of risk-adjusted-return analysis before. Your last financial advisor told you to just invest and then forget about it, right? After all, nobody can "time the market," and you're not going to get out of your investments whatever happens, so why worry yourself with short-term results when you don't need the cash in the account for years and years in the future?

I'll assume you went off and did your homework and came back with terrible MAR ratios that were much less than 0.5, or even much less than zero. And your CAGRs are probably nowhere near the "standard" 10% everybody talks about, and you most likely have drawdowns that are at least 50%, if not closer to 60%. If this is not the case, then you're already an investment guru (or you did your number crunching wrong), and you don't need to read the rest of this chapter.

If the only result of reading this chapter is that you finally understand whether you're getting paid for the risk you are taking in your investments accounts, then all your hard work understanding this information so far will have paid off big time. You may not be inclined to actively manage your investments yourself, but if you stop doing what doesn't work and put that cash into your emergency fund or savings as described in the previous two chapters, you'll be much better off than if you do nothing.

Let's assume you now realize that you're getting a terrible result from your current investment management methods (if you can call what you've been doing before "a method"). Before we get into the details about managing your investments, I need to make a couple of things very clear:

- For most people, it is not appropriate or rational to take uncontrolled risk in an investment account, with little chance of a decent return—especially with your retirement savings.
- There is no way that I (or anyone) can show you how to achieve the same performance that a full-time professional money manager can achieve in your investment accounts, even if you do put in the hour per week or so of effort into a spreadsheet, as this chapter will show you how to do.

For these reasons it's important that I talk about *not* actively managing your investment accounts before I talk about how to manage them effectively.

Don't Even Think About Trying to Manage Your Retirement Account

I've shown earlier in this book that FARCE[1] doesn't work, and if that's what you're doing in your retirement or investment accounts, then you're likely going to be disappointed when you retire. If your employer is making matching contributions, then you should treat these as your "return on investment." This "free money," along with the deferral of income taxes until you retire, should mean that your account grows faster than inflation.

If you think about this for a minute, you should reach a conclusion: you should put your entire retirement account into a money market fund to minimize risk. Yes, you'll get a tiny return, but you'll pay the lowest fees and have the lowest chance of losing money. Note that your plan sponsor, your employer, your friends and family, or anyone else you mention this to will think you are crazy to give up the long-term "10%-a-year return" that so many investment advisors point to as a bedrock financial fact. Don't even attempt to explain your rationale—just tell them to read this book.

As for your other investment accounts, where nobody is doing any matching contributions on your behalf, then you should seriously consider whether there is a better place for you to apply that cash than the shark-infested waters of the financial industry. If you are still going to risk it, then make sure you have a sound investment method that has a reasonable chance of success. This is what the rest of this chapter is about.

Mr. and Mrs. Fit Visit a Casino

Mr. and Mrs. Fit decide to take a vacation to Las Vegas and go see some shows. While they are there, they decide to visit a casino on the main strip. The casino happens to be hosting a huge poker event, and the Fits decide to participate. Mr. Fit read a book about Texas hold 'em a while ago, and Mrs. Fit has a natural talent with probabilities and numbers.

To enter the tournament, all they have to do is "buy in" for an initial $10,000. If they lose that, then they can buy more chips any time they like—they just have to pony up more cash. The casino takes a small fee (called a rake) from the pot for every hand played. They can also cash out their chips any time they like and get their remaining cash back.

---

[1] For those of you who don't remember, it stands for Faithful Annual Rebalancing of Common ETFs.

This is a huge tournament, and there are about 1,000 players at any one time. The average buy-in is about $10,000. Mr. and Mrs. Fit are just like 95% of the players—amateurs playing for fun, people on vacation looking for a thrill, people who have read some books on poker and think they can employ simple strategies to make some consistent, easy money. There are even some people who have taken their retirement savings and think they can consistently increase their chip stack by "playing the odds" and only betting when they have a "good" hand.

The other 5% of the players in the tournament are full-time professional poker players. They play day-in, day-out and are experts at reading the other players, managing their chip stack, and knowing when to bluff and when to fold. They can easily calculate probabilities in their heads. They can also do some pretty neat tricks with poker chips since they are so used to handling them, and they always know exactly how many chips they have in play and how many are in the pot.

Mr. and Mrs. Fit start playing conservatively and make only small bets. The casino gets paid because it takes its fee for each hand played. So the number of chips in play is slowly decreasing, but not really fast enough for anyone to notice. Mr. Fit notices that there is one player at his table that seems to be doing well, and a significant amount of chips seem to be accumulating in front of him. Other people at Mr. Fit's table are either quitting because they are out of chips, or buying in again if they have some cash remaining.

No matter what Mr. Fit does, it seems that the "good" player always folds when Mr. Fit has a good hand and makes a large bet, calls or raises when Mr. Fit bluffs, and makes a bet when he has poor cards. It's almost like the other player knows what Mr. Fit's cards are, even though he is very careful to keep them concealed when he looks at them.

Mrs. Fit is doing a little better because of her superior probability, statistics, and number skills. She is managing to bet only when the odds are in her favor and not risk a lot of money, even when she thinks her opponents have inferior hands. However, effective chip-stack management and playing the odds well can only slow down the gradual flow of Mrs. Fit's chips to the casino and the superior players in the tournament.

The Fits play for a few hours, lose 20% of their chips, and decide to cash out. Mr. Fit decides he needs to read some more books on good poker strategy before coming back and trying again next year—if only he had the right betting technique and playing strategy, he could clean up. What Mr. Fit doesn't realize is that it's impossible to make money in this environment unless you're either the casino taking the rake, or one of the small number of full-time professional players who consistently end up with the amateurs' chips before the casino takes them, again via its rake.

If this sounds familiar, it's because it is a great analogy for the way the financial industry works.

If You Do Want to Manage Your Own Investment Accounts, Don't Use FARCE

If you've read this far and you have followed all the rest of the advice in this book, then you're probably pretty financially savvy and also pretty adept at making a spreadsheet program work for you. You have an emergency fund in precious metals, you've put your savings into currencies or ETFs depending on the prevailing interest rate environment, and you have your retirement account funds "safe" in a money market account.

However, because your finances are now fit and you're making more cash every month than you spend, you have more savings than you're comfortable with simply rebalancing on a quarterly basis. Because upon scrutiny, if you did the homework I mention in the previous section, it probably hasn't worked out that well. You want a chance of a better return by taking more risk in a controlled manner. The rest of this chapter is the best way to go about doing this if you don't know any good money managers who will take your cash and manage it full-time for a reasonable fee. The good money managers are few and far between, and even if you can find one, they probably don't want the hassle of managing a load of relatively small accounts (small to *them* anyway). As a result, they often have high minimum-investment requirements or only take institutional funds from other financial firms.

If you have $100,000 but don't have the passion, inclination, time, or technical skills to manage it yourself, then drop me a line and I can refer you to someone who implements the techniques I describe in the rest of this chapter for a small annual asset management fee.

Whatever you do, though, please take heed of these warnings:

- Don't use FARCE to manage your investment accounts.
- Don't use dollar cost averaging to manage your investment accounts.

If you don't understand why, just take a closer look at Chapter 2 and Figure 5-1 later in this chapter.

"Trading" vs. "Investing"

If you buy mutual funds in your retirement account or other brokerage account and intend to hold on to them for the long term, you're investing, not trading, right? Wrong! You're just trading without any predefined exit strategy. There is only one reason to buy any financial instrument—because you want to sell it again later when the price has gone up. You can't buy groceries with Microsoft stock, so you must sell it first and turn it back into currency before you can spend the proceeds.

In my opinion, this means that everyone is a trader, not an investor. You're an investor if you lend a startup company money in exchange for a share of the company or a slice of future revenues. Then you don't technically need an exit strategy—in this case, meaning a method to limit risk rather than a way to cash out. Either the company will succeed and you'll get paid, or it will fail and you'll lose your initial investment.

Why am I making this seemingly irrelevant distinction? It's because there are six major components to a sound and complete *trading* strategy. So, for example, if you're a buy-and-hold investor, what you're really doing is trading with a system that only has one defined component: the entry signal. This would be like playing in a poker tournament and only using one rule: "I'll bet half of my chips if I have a pair of aces in the hole." In other words, you bet only in one instance, letting the chips fall where they may. And you can bet the chips will fall into the hands of the house and other players. How long do you think you would last if that was the only rule you had?

Here are the six components of a complete trading approach:

1. Market selection
2. Instrument filter
3. Setup conditions
4. Entry signal
5. Position sizing
6. Exit strategy

You may be looking at this list and thinking, "Wow, that looks like a lot of work; I don't want to be a full-time investment manager." Yes, it's true, good trading is not as simple as doing a quarterly rebalancing of your portfolio. But you have to ask yourself one question: "Am I happy with the performance of my investment account with the methods I've been using and the time and effort I've put in?" If the answer is a big, fat no, then ask yourself one more question: "Am I prepared to put in a bit of effort up front in order to understand and implement a much better method for managing my investment accounts? A method that will take a maximum of an hour per week to manage once it's completed, and will give me a better chance of a good risk-adjusted return *for the rest of my investing life?*"If the answers is no, then you don't need to read the rest of this chapter, and you should close your investment accounts and either put the cash into your emergency fund or take an emergency vacation to somewhere hot and sunny.

So, if you're still with me, I'll now deal briefly with each component of a complete trading method. Note that this is not a complete guide to building trading programs—it's meant to show you how little of a complete approach a buy-and-hold investor really has, and why the results most people achieve are so predictably terrible (or should that be terribly predictable?). Occasionally, I'll relate the component to your retirement account, since in most cases the major decisions about how you manage this type of investment account have already been made for you, or your choices are severely restricted.

Market Selection

Market selection determines what markets you will trade, and in turn defines the complete universe of instruments that you will consider as potentially tradable. For example, you could decide that your chosen market will be all equities listed on the New York Stock Exchange (NYSE), National Association of Securities Dealers Automated Quotation System (NASDAQ), and American Stock Exchange (AMEX). In your retirement account, market selection has probably been decided for you—it's simply the list of mutual funds your plan sponsor chose as investment options. By the way, this choice is normally limited to less than ten, simply so that you're more likely to make a choice—any choice. Studies have shown that if more options are provided, there is an increased probability that the participant (i.e., you) will choose the money market fund because the participant can't make a decision. This is the last place the company running your retirement plan wants you to put your cash, simply because their fees are the lowest in this fund. They want you to allocate to the other funds that have higher fees.

If you are going to trade your own capital, make sure it's in an environment that offers the biggest choice of markets and does not artificially constrain your tradable universe. Interactive Brokers is a good choice since they offer access to virtually all global electronic markets and their fees are very low.[2]

Instrument Filter

The instrument filter determines which instruments in the chosen markets are suitable for trading right now. Again, this decision has already been made for you in your retirement account. When choosing instruments to trade, there are four main factors to consider:

- *Liquidity*: How much volume is there in this instrument?
- *Spread*: What is the difference between the current buying (bid) and selling (offer) price?
- *Fees*: How much will you have to pay to enter and exit positions?
- *Slippage*: How different will your actual fulfillment price be from the price quoted when you enter your order?

Not all instruments are liquid enough to trade without large spread and slippage, and the fees may be high, which could all lead to significant implementation costs. These eat into your potential profit and amplify any losses. All an instrument filter does is take the complete universe of all instruments in a particular market and tells you exactly which ones should be considered for trading *right now*. This means that your liquid universe can change on a daily basis. You must have a method of reevaluating it periodically. It's not a "pick once and forget about it" type of thing, like the approach you used in your retirement account.

For example, if your chosen market is US ETFs listed on the NYSE, then you could have an instrument filter that says you will only include ETFs that are in the top tenth percentile measured by average daily volume (ADV) over the last 30 days. Most financial sites have a method of listing ETFs by various criteria, including volume, so it should not be a problem to find a ranked list that makes it simple to only choose instruments that are in the top 100, or top 10%.[3]

---

[2] I am not affiliated with Interactive Brokers, and am simply mentioning them as the most suitable choice I have currently found for the implementation of the methods contained in this book.

[3] The ETF center on Yahoo Finance has a suitable ranking tool. Go to Investing, and then ETFs, choose View ETFs by Volume, and then rank by "Volume (3 mo Avg)."

Setup Conditions

Setup conditions are conditions that must be true for a trade to be considered. An example would be whether the volume today is sufficient for you to enter a position. Even though the chosen instruments in your market may have been liquid (had high volume) when you selected them, they may not have sufficient volume *right now* to consider a trade.

Again, if you're talking about your retirement account, then setup conditions have already been decided for you—any time is a good time to invest, and typically your plan will be set up with monthly contributions and an automatic allocation to your chosen funds. In a sound trading system, not all instruments in your liquid universe are good candidates for trading all the time—setup conditions tell you when you should be considering a trade in a particular instrument, and importantly, when you should not.

Entry Signal

Entry signal determines the specific conditions under which a buy order (or a sell order if you're shorting something) is generated. In your retirement account, the entry signal is, "Buy $X per month based on your predetermined allocation to the funds in your plan." A valid entry signal should take into account the prevailing trend of the instrument being considered, and not just default to "buy every month"—as is done in your retirement account. If something has been dropping like a stone for the last six months, what makes you think it's a good idea to go ahead and buy it right now? Oh, that dollar cost averaging thing I covered in Chapter 2, right? Again, it's probably not a good idea to ignore the prevailing trend and go ahead and buy anyway?

Of all the concepts about the way markets work that are endlessly argued over by all the participants in the market, there are only two that you really need to understand:

- Momentum
- Inertia

In physics, momentum is defined as the tendency for a body that is in motion to stay in motion unless acted upon by an external force. Inertia is the tendency for a body that is at rest to stay at rest unless acted upon by an external force. In trading, momentum means that if the price of an instrument is moving in a particular direction, then it will often continue to move in that direction *unless something changes*. Inertia means that if the price of an instrument is going nowhere, then it will often continue to go nowhere *unless something changes.*

The practical implications of these concepts are pretty simple to understand:

- Buy things that are going up.
- Sell things that are going down.
- Don't buy or sell things that are going sideways.

Position Sizing

Position sizing is how much to buy or sell at any point in time, and depends on several factors that I will describe in detail later in this chapter. For most people in a retirement account, once again, this is predetermined—you will buy as much as possible based on your contribution and your employer's matching contribution. If you were playing in a poker tournament, then this position-sizing algorithm is basically "go all-in every time," which means bet all your chips every time you play a hand. As the saying goes in poker, "Going all-in works every time . . . except once."

Taking 100% risk by "investing" 100% of your cash is insane, especially when your exit strategy amounts to "Hold on for dear life, whatever happens." A sound position-sizing algorithm limits the risk you will take on each position so that your maximum risk is kept within your tolerances. Did anyone ever talk to you about maximum expected drawdown when you chose your allocation percentages in your retirement account? No, I didn't think so.

Position sizing is the part of your trading system that determines two things:

- Your likely CAGR
- Your likely maximum drawdown

If either of these is important to you, then you better make sure you have a good understanding of the implications of any particular position-sizing method, rather than just buying as much as you can.

Exit Strategy

The exit strategy is the set of rules that determine when you will get out of a position. After position sizing, this component of a trading system is the most important and basically determines your expectation.

If I said you could toss a fair coin and I would pay you $1 for heads and you would pay me $2 for tails, then the expectations would be:

- 50% chance of a $1 loss for me
- 50% chance of a $2 loss for you

My expectations would be:

(Probability of a Win * Win Amount) – (Probability of a Loss * Loss Amount)

Which works out to the following:

$$(0.5 * \$2) - (0.5 * \$1) = 1.0 - 0.5 = 0.5$$

This means that if I played the game with you, I would win 50 cents per turn on average—a positive expectation for me, and an equal and opposite negative expectation for you. Whether you're playing a positive or negative expectation game with your investment accounts depends primarily on your exit strategy. What's your exit strategy in your retirement account? Don't have one? You probably do, but it may be along the lines of "Cash out when I'm 60 years old." Do such exit rules help you manage risk, keep losing positions small, let winners grow big, or create a positive expectation? Nope.

And if you're using periodic portfolio rebalancing, your exit strategy basically says: "Sell things that have gone up and buy things that have gone down with the proceeds."

This is the opposite of what "good" trading looks like: "Let winners run, and cut losers short."

Putting It All Together

I'm not going to pretend I can give you a complete trading method for all major instrument types that you can implement in a few hours a month using a spreadsheet and some delayed market data. What I can do is show you a much, much better way of managing your investment accounts than the typical "buy and hold with periodic rebalancing" that you're probably currently using.

I can also show you what your results would have looked like over the last, say, eight years using this method so you can compare them to the actual results you have achieved using traditional methods.

Let me make it clear again that it's risk-adjusted return depicted by the MAR ratio that's important—not simply CAGR. Figure 5-1 shows the baseline we're trying to improve upon. You may recognize this chart from Chapter 2. If your plan sponsor actually provided you with a chart that showed actual returns and drawdowns, rather than simply the total value of your account including your contributions, it would probably look a lot like the following chart over the last few years. The chart is of a simple annual rebalancing model of a diversified portfolio consisting of equities, bonds, and emerging markets. The ETFs in the portfolio are:

- *SPY*: SPDR S&P 500 ETF
- *TLT*: iShares Barclays 20+ Year Treasury Bond
- *EFA*: iShares Trust MSCI EAFE Index (Europe, Australasia, and Far East equities)

The account starts with $100,000 and has a 2% annual fee applied to it.

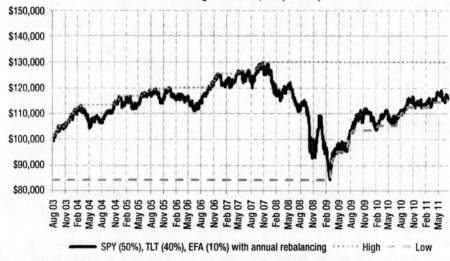

Figure 5-1. Annual rebalancing of a diversified portfolio, August 2003 to July 2011

Not very impressive, is it? I don't need to go into how pathetic these results are, because I covered that in Chapter 2. How about Figure 5-2—does this look a little more like it?

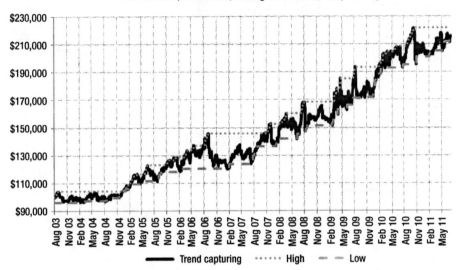

Figure 5-2. Trend capturing applied to a diversified portfolio, August 2003 to July 2011, with 2% annual fee

I've included the same 2% annual fee so you can directly compare it to the previous chart. I would call these results acceptable for an approach that could be managed on your own using a diversified portfolio of ETFs (including some inverse ETFs) and a spreadsheet with delayed market data. The approach attempts to capture trends in price as, and when, they occur, and does not use any kind of periodic rebalancing.

Figure 5-3 shows the same method with no annual fee, which would represent the kind of results that could be achieved if you do it yourself. If the results with the 2% annual fee look good to you, and you just can't be bothered to do the hard work to manage an account yourself for the kind of improvement that's possible, then just get in touch with me and I will refer you to a financial advisor I know. This financial advisor is implementing a version of the method I describe in detail later in this chapter, and currently takes accounts of at least $100,000 but only charges a small annual fee based on total assets.[4]

---

[4] I currently receive no compensation for such referrals.

Figure 5-3. Trend capturing applied to a diversified portfolio, August 2003 to July 2011, with no annual fee

As you can see from the last chart, doing it yourself (assuming you don't mess up, of course), your account balance would be just about $20,000 bigger at the end of the period.

A Simplified Trend-Capturing Method

Now that I've gotten your interest with what I consider to be good results, it's time to give you a few warnings:

- Achieving these results requires accurate and consistent implementation of the trading method. No skipping a trade you don't like, no sizing a trade twice as big because it's going to be a huge winner, and no taking a six-month vacation and forgetting to look at your account. If you can't accurately and consistently implement the method, then don't bother—you'll end up worse off than using FARCE.
- The methods presented here require more time and effort than most normal people are willing to spend managing their investment accounts.

- There is no guarantee that future results will look exactly like the past results. However, there is a much better chance of future results being acceptable compared to FARCE in my opinion, so it's worth the risk.

The method I describe next is a simplified version of what I and other professional traders use that is easier to manage while still providing good results. The results for this version are shown in Figure 5-4.

Simplified Trend Capturing, Starting Value $100,000, No Annual Fee, from 08/08/2003 to 07/18/2011, CAGR%=10.67%, Maximum DD=20.63%, MAR=0.517, Ending Value $217,907 (117.91%)

Figure 5-4. Simplified trend capturing applied to a diversified portfolio, August 2003 to July 2011, with no annual fee

As you can see, the CAGR is lower and the max DD is higher, but that is the price one pays for using a method that is simple to implement and doesn't require full-time babysitting.

So, with that out of the way, let me tell you the exact rules you can use to implement the simplified trend-capturing method yourself.

Market Selection

Plan to buy US ETFs listed on the NYSE and AMEX.

Most people are familiar with equities (stocks), but investing in individual companies has some drawbacks—the price can be very volatile, and if the company gets into trouble, the shareholders are the last in line to get any cash back. Anyone remember Enron or Worldcom? In fact, of the 12 companies on the original Dow Jones Industrial Average, only 1 still exists today (General Electric).

For this reason, it's better to invest in ETFs that represent ownership of a collection of underlying instruments rather than a single company, so you get "built-in" diversification. Another advantage is that ETFs trade just like equities (they are priced in real time and trade on regular exchanges), so they are easy to buy or sell in any regular brokerage account.

Instrument Filter

Rank the top 50 ETFs by dollar volume traded and choose a noncorrelated list from this set that includes some inverse funds. Noncorrelated in this case means that the holdings of each ETF should not have much overlap and should not be based on a similar index, industry, or sector.

Inverse funds are ETFs that are designed to move in the opposite direction to some other fund or index so they can be used to simulate going short in an account where selling short is not allowed.[5] This means that you can benefit from uptrends as well as downtrends, rather than only being able to make money when things are going up in price.

There are many web sites that can list and rank ETFs quickly and easily. I like to use the ETF Center in Yahoo! Finance, but any source that can be easily loaded into your spreadsheet program so you can sort it will work. Table 5.1 shows a list of ETFs ranked by descending average daily volume.

---

[5] Going short, or "shorting," is a trading technique in which you borrow securities from your broker, sell them, and receive the proceeds. Then you have to buy back the securities at some point in the future in order to return them to your broker. In this way, you can benefit from a drop in price if you are able to buy the securities back for less than you received when you sold them. Shorting of securities is not allowed in US retirement accounts.

Table 5-1. Example ETF List Ranked by Volume

Name	Symbol	Volume
SPDR S&P 500	SPY	170,962,000
iShares Silver Trust	SLV	72,034,000
Financial Select Sector SPDR	XLF	67,204,000
iShares MSCI Emerging Markets Index	EEM	61,268,400
PowerShares QQQ	QQQ	60,377,900
iShares Russell 2000 Index	IWM	60,075,700
iShares MSCI Japan Index	EWJ	52,765,600
ProShares UltraShort S&P500	SDS	23,673,300
iPath S&P 500 VIX Short-Term Futures ETN	VXX	22,735,200
Vanguard MSCI Emerging Markets ETF	VWO	20,913,100
Energy Select Sector SPDR	XLE	20,550,300
Direxion Daily Financial Bull 3X Shares	FAS	19,390,100
iShares MSCI EAFE Index	EFA	18,649,400
Industrial Select Sector SPDR	XLI	18,163,000
United States Oil	USO	17,110,200
iShares FTSE China 25 Index Fund	FXI	15,893,900
SPDR Gold Shares	GLD	15,579,000
United States Natural Gas	UNG	14,989,800
Materials Select Sector SPDR	XLB	14,288,400
ProShares UltraShort Silver	ZSL	13,908,300
iShares MSCI Brazil Index	EWZ	13,525,200
Direxion Daily Small Cap Bear 3X Shares	TZA	13,456,500
ProShares Ultra S&P500	SSO	13,163,300
iShares MSCI Taiwan Index	EWT	12,166,300
Semiconductor HOLDRs	SMH	11,434,600
SPDR S&P Retail	XRT	11,222,800

Name	Symbol	Volume
Technology Select Sector SPDR	XLK	10,722,600
Direxion Daily Financial Bear 3X Shares	FAZ	10,298,700
ProShares UltraShort 20+ Year Treasury	TBT	10,284,500
Market Vectors Gold Miners ETF	GDX	10,086,300

In the table, the ETFs have been ranked in descending order by three-month ADV.

The next step is to go through the list and decide exactly which ETFs will be included in your "tradable universe." Go down the list and put a check mark by any noncorrelated ETFs—ETFs that do not represent the same main category as any already on your list. Once you have at least 20 ETFs on your list, it is fine to stop. This process should be repeated at least yearly in order to make sure you are always trading the most liquid ETFs that currently exist.

After looking at about the top 60 ETFs, I came up with a list of the 20 I'd invest in (Table 5-2).

Table 5-2. Top 20 Diversified, Most Liquid ETFs

Symbol	Name
SPY	SPDR S&P 500
SLV	iShares Silver Trust
XLF	Financial Select Sector SPYDR
EEM	iShares Emerging Markets
QQQ	PowerShares QQQ
IWM	iShares Russell 2000
EWJ	iShares MSCI Japan Index
TLT	iShares Barclays 20+ Year Treasury Bond
FXI	iShares FTSE China 25 Index Fund
GLD	SPDR Gold Trust

Symbol	Name
XLE	Energy Select Sector SPDR
EWZ	iShares MSCI Brazil Index
EWT	iShares MSCI Taiwan Index
EWH	iShares MSCI Hong Kong Index
EWG	iShares MSCI Germany Index
RSX	Market Vectors Russia ETF
EWA	iShares MSCI Australia Index
EWC	iShares MSCI Canada Index
UUP	PowerShares DB US Dollar Index Bullish
EPI	WisdomTree India Earnings

All I did was start at the top and skip any ETFs where there was considerable overlap with one already on the list. For example, USO, United States Oil, was eliminated since XLE, Energy Select Sector SPDR, was already on the list. And GDX, Market Vectors Gold Miners ETF, was not included because GLD, SPDR Gold Trust, was. Don't fret too much about whether something overlaps or not—look at the fund category and use common sense. It's better to skip something that isn't correlated than accidentally include something that is. There are hundreds of liquid ETFs to choose from, and you only need a selection of 20. Include some inverse funds, too, so you can take advantage of drops in the market. It's ideal if all of the funds you choose have inverse funds to pair with; however, everything will still be fine if approximately half of the funds you choose have an inverse.

This means that if you end up with 20 main funds, 10 of which have an inverse, then your complete portfolio list will be 30 funds in total. Also, it's important to point out that you will never have a position in a fund *and its inverse at the same time*, so the maximum number of simultaneous positions you can ever have is the total number of main funds. The only real criteria are that the fund be liquid (so you can buy and sell easily without affecting the price) and have little overlap with what's already on your list.

The next step is to identify whether there is an inverse fund for each of the ETFs so you can potentially have a position in a particular category depending on whether it's currently going up or down. For the 20 ETFs on the list, Table 5-3 shows those that have inverse funds.

Table 5-3. Common ETFs with Inverse Funds

Symbol	Name	Inverse Fund
SPY	SPDR S&P 500	SH
SLV	iShares Silver Trust	PSQ
XLF	Financial Select Sector SPYDR	SKF
EEM	iShares Emerging Markets	EUM
QQQ	PowerShares QQQ	QID
IWM	iShares Russell 2000	RWM
EWJ	iShares MSCI Japan Index	EWV
TLT	iShares Barclays 20+ Year Treasury Bond	TBT
FXI	iShares FTSE China 25 Index Fund	FXP
GLD	SPDR Gold Trust	UGL

I quickly found the inverse ETFs by doing a web search for "Inverse ETFs." If you are really serious about investing, then you could also do a correlation study on the historical data to make sure that the inverse ETFs really do what they are supposed to—that is, move in the opposite direction to their specified "twin." Since we are only concerned about trend-capturing moves in these ETFs, it doesn't really matter if a particular fund is an exact inverse correlation, as long as it has the potential to go up when the twin fund is going down.

Note that some inverse funds are designed to have more than a 100% negative correlation—they are designed to move two (or more times) in the opposite direction of their twin fund. For example, in a 3-times fund, a 1% down move in the noninverse fund should result in a 3% up move in the inverse fund.

These are typically called ultra-short funds to indicate that they don't have just a one-to-one negative correlation. As you will see when we get to the position-sizing section, investing in ultra-short ETFs is not a problem as long as you decrease your position size to take account of the increased volatility of these funds. In fact, if you can take the desired amount of risk but have a smaller position (based on the actual value of the shares), then an ultra-short fund is more capital efficient than a regular ETF. It takes up less cash to implement the same amount of risk.

Again, a check should be done on at least an annual basis to see if any new inverse funds have been created that match the other funds on the list so they can be included in your portfolio.

Setup Conditions

Once you have selected the ETFs you want to buy and sell, there are a couple of conditions that must be met before you actually buy. These are:

1. You have some cash left.

2. You do not already have 20 open positions.

The first criterion is pretty obvious: if you have already used up all available cash in your investment account, then you can't put any more positions on until something is sold to free up new investment capital.

The second criterion is there to limit the total amount of risk you are willing to take, and depends on two things that will be covered in the "Position Sizing" section, which follows:

*   How much of your account are you prepared to lose in total?
*   How much are you prepared to lose on each individual position?

Remember that return and risk go hand in hand, so the more you are prepared to lose, the better chance of a bigger return you will have. Obviously the opposite is also true—if you aim for higher returns, then you will experience bigger drawdowns in your account. You should always concentrate on managing the risk and controlling losses first—the return will take care of itself if you accurately implement your trading method.

Entry Signal

Based on the concept of momentum mentioned earlier in the chapter, what you want to do is buy things that are going up and attempt to capture part of a trend when one develops. Therefore, our entry signal is simply a specific definition of what "going up" means. Here is that definition:

An increase in price over the last ten days is greater than three times the ATR(10)

As you can see from the definition, the entry signal has two components:

*   How volatile the recent price range has been (represented by the ATR)
*   How much the price has changed from close to close over the same period

ATR is the *average true range*, which will be explained in the next few paragraphs, and the number in parentheses is the number of days. If the price move is greater than three times the ATR(10), then the move is "significant." The price move over the same period is simply the difference between the closing price yesterday and ten days ago.

Whether a price move can be considered a significant up move or not depends on how volatile the price of the ETF really is. For example, let's assume we have an ETF that moves up (or down) by $1 per day on average, over the last ten days. A price move of $2.50 over the last ten days could not be considered significant; it only represents a total move of 50% of the daily range (50 cents) per day. Conversely, if price has moved up by $3 or more over the same period, then it could be considered significant, since this represents a move that is 60% of the total daily range in one direction.

It's important to think only in ratios of some measure of volatility, rather than absolute price moves. This means that any definition of significant price move must include an estimation of how volatile the daily price has been recently. This is when the ATR, developed by J. Welles Wilder, is useful.

With stocks, the *range* is simply the high price minus the low price for the day. But this calculation does not take into account the difference between the previous day's closing price and today's opening price. The *true range* for the day takes this into account by using the following formula:

True Range = The Maximum of (Daily Range, High Distance, Low Distance)

This means that you will use the highest value out of the three choices (daily range, high distance, and low distance). Here's what those terms mean:

- *Daily range*: Today's high minus today's low
- *High distance*: Absolute value of today's high minus the previous day's close
- *Low distance*: Absolute value of today's low minus the previous day's close

The ATR is a simple arithmetic average (mean) of the true range over some defined number of days. In our case, we will use ten days. Table 5-4 shows the ATR calculations for the ETF SPY over the last ten days. In this case, the ATR(10) is 1.52, which means that on average, the price of SPY went up (or down) by $1.52 per day over the last ten days.

Table 5-4. Ten-Day ATR Calculation for SPY

	A	B	C	D	E	F	G	H	I
1	Day Reference	Close Price	High Price	Low Price	Day Range	High Distance	Low Distance	True Range	ATR (10)
2									
3	-11	134.44							
4	-10	135.08	135.36	133.39	1.97	0.92	1.05	1.97	
5	-9	134.04	135.34	133.56	1.78	0.26	1.52	1.78	
6	-8	133.19	134.61	132.97	1.64	0.57	1.07	1.64	
7	-7	133.17	133.35	132.12	1.23	0.16	1.07	1.23	
8	-6	134.36	134.50	132.95	1.55	1.33	0.22	1.55	
9	-5	134.68	135.03	133.94	1.09	0.67	0.42	1.09	
10	-4	133.61	134.68	133.36	1.32	0.00	1.32	1.32	
11	-3	132.06	133.65	131.59	2.06	0.04	2.02	2.06	
12	-2	131.95	132.73	131.70	1.03	0.67	0.36	1.03	
13	-1	132.39	132.94	131.38	1.56	0.99	0.57	1.56	1.52

The spreadsheet formulas for the calculations in Table 5-4 are shown in Table 5-5.

Table 5-5. Spreadsheet Formulas for Table 5-4

Cell	Formula	Value
E13	=C13-D13	1.56
F13	=ABS(C13-B12)	0.99
G13	=ABS(D13-B12)	0.57
H13	=MAX(E13,F13,G13)	1.56
I13	=AVERAGE(H4:H13)	1.52

Therefore, based on our rule that three times the ten-day ATR is a significant price move, you would enter a position in SPY if it moved up by 3 * $1.52, which is $4.56 over ten days.

Adding an additional column to the spreadsheet, you can easily calculate the price move (close to close) over the last ten days and see if it is more than three times the ATR(10) for the same period, as shown in Table 5-6.

Table 5-6. Price Move in ATR(10) over Last Ten Days

	A	B	C	D	E
1	Day Reference	Close Price	Price Move	ATR(10)	ATR(10) Multiple
2					
3	-11	134.44			
4	-10	135.08			
5	-9	134.04			
6	-8	133.19			
7	-7	133.17			
8	-6	134.36			
9	-5	134.68			
10	-4	133.61			
11	-3	132.06			
12	-2	131.95			
13	-1	132.39	-2.05	1.52	-1.35

Again, the spreadsheet formulas for Table 5-6 are shown in Table 5-7.

Table 5-7. Spreadsheet Formulas for Table 5-6

Cell	Formula	Value
C13	=B13-B3	-2.05
E13	=C13/D13	-1.35

As you can see from the ATR(10) Multiple column in Table 5-6, the price has actually gone down by 1.35 times the ATR(10) over the ten-day period. If the price had gone up by a multiple of 3 or more of the ATR(10), then that would be a signal to enter a position in this ETF as long as you didn't already have a position in it or in the inverse fund. Remember, never take a position in an ETF if you already have a position in its mate.

In order to check for entry signals in all the ETFs on your list, it's a good idea to build a spreadsheet that automatically grabs the historical price data, calculates the ATR(10), and works out whether you have any entry signals to take.

The product I use to get the historical data into Excel is called XLQ, from a company called QMatix.[6] This means that your spreadsheet will automatically update each time it is run, and you won't have to manually type in all the historical prices. Manual typing is obviously impractical when you have a list of 20 ETFs plus the inverse ETFs to update—unless you're a data entry addict.

Position Sizing

Once your setup conditions are fulfilled and you have a valid entry signal on one (or more) of the ETFs on your list, it's time to actually buy some shares. The question is, "How many shares do you buy?" Here is the formula to use:

> 2% of account net liquidation value (NLV) based on a
> 10 times ATR(50) risk per share.

The risk per share in the formula means the difference between the current price and the price at which you would exit if this were not a winning trade. How to determine this exit price is covered in the "Exit Strategy" section.

The purpose of your position-sizing calculation is to tell you exactly how many shares to buy based on the following pieces of information:

- The current NLV of your account
- The current ATR(50) of the ETF
- The percentage of your account you are prepared to risk on each position

---

[6] The QMatix web site is http://qmatix.com. There is a fully functional free trial of XLQ that can be downloaded from the web site.

The NLV of your account is a simple calculation that all brokerage statements include. You can either use the value from your last statement, or you can use the online access to your account to get an up-to-date value. The NLV is simply the current value of all the positions in your account, including any cash positions, accrued interest, dividends, and so on. It represents what your account would be worth (in base currency) if everything were liquidated at current prices.

In the same way that you calculated the 10-day ATR for the entry signal, you want to use a slightly longer timeframe calculation (50 days in this case) as a proxy for what volatility may be when you are in the position. Volatility may go up or down after you've put a position on, and our exit strategy will react to those changes, but for right now, the most recent volatility is the best estimate you have for what the price range will be like for this particular ETF.

The risk per trade in this case is going to be 2% of your account. Note that this does not mean you will enter a position that costs 2% of your NLV. It means that if this position is exited at your stop-loss point (which is covered in the "Exit Strategy" section), then you will suffer a 2% loss of your current account NLV.

The sizing calculation is in two steps. First we determine how much the risk per share will be

Risk Per Share = 10 * the 50-Day ATR

Let's say that in this case the 50-day ATR is the same as the 10-day ATR in the entry signal example (that's 1.52). This means the risk per share calculation would be as follows:

Risk Per Share = 10 * $1.52 = $15.20

Using the SPY example, this means we would be risking $15.20 per share for this position. Note that if 10 times the ATR(50) is bigger than the current price of the ETF, then you cannot take a position in this ETF. The stop price (based on the risk per share) would be negative. This particular trade should be skipped under these circumstances, and you should just wait for the next entry signal.

Next, you need to work out how much you are going to risk on this trade using our risk per trade of 2%. Let's say your current NLV is $100,000.

Risk on This Trade = Risk-per-Trade Percentage * NLV

Risk on This Trade = 2% * $100,000 = $2,000

We know how much we will be risking per share ($15.20) and we know what the total risk for this trade will be ($2,000), so the number of shares to buy is simply the following:

Shares to Buy = Total Risk / Risk per Share

Shares to Buy = $2000 / $15.20 = 131 (rounded down)

Note that you can't buy fractional shares in ETFs as you can with a mutual fund, so you need to round the number of shares down to an integer value (131 in this case). If you're the kind of investor that likes round numbers, then you can round down to the nearest 10 or 100 shares, but since ETFs are very liquid, it should not be a problem buying and selling odd lots.

That's it—the calculation is identical in all cases and is designed to risk a fixed percentage of your current NLV on each trade. In this particular example, if the current price of SPY were $132.39, then buying 131 shares would represent a position with a total value of $17,343 (131 shares at $132.39 per share). Note that this has two implications:

- You would only be able to have a maximum of five positions in your $100,000 account if each position "cost" over $17,000.
- The amount of risk you are taking on each position ($2,000 in this example) is not the same as the value or cost of the position since you will exit before the price goes to zero (see the "Exit Strategy" section).

Since the cost of each position is determined by how volatile an ETF is compared to its current price, ETFs that are more volatile (relative to their price) actually require a smaller position to take the same amount of risk. This means that "ultra," or leveraged, ETFs are actually more capital efficient than nonleveraged ones, and should be preferred if you have entry signals in more than one ETF but don't have enough capital to put all the positions on.

Capital efficiency in this case is determined by the following formula:

10-Day ATR / Closing Price As a Percentage

So, for SPY in our example, this would be:

1.52 / 132.39 * 100 = 1.15% (rounded to two decimal places)

Typically, capital efficiency is between 1% and 3%, with higher capital efficiency being better since you will be able to put on more positions with the same amount of capital and get better diversification in your portfolio. It's a good idea to do this calculation in your spreadsheet program and then rank the ETFs by descending capital efficiency percent so you can see which ones are better.

Why Only 2% Risk per Trade?

You may be thinking that risking *only* 2% of your account on any single position doesn't sound like much, especially when you're only going to have a maximum of 20 positions (assuming you don't run out of cash to implement them). But let me show you a simple chart (Figure 5-5) that I show to all my trading clients at some point during trading system development.

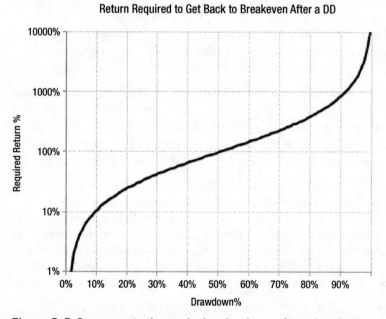

Figure 5-5. Return required to get back to breakeven after a drawdown

As you can see from the figure, the graph is approximately linear up to about 11%. This means that if you lose 11% of your account, you need to make approximately 11% return on what you have left to get back to where you started. The real action is further to the right of the chart. If you lose 50% of your account, then you have to make a 100% return (i.e., double) the cash you have left just to get back to where you started. The ratio of return to drawdown has gone from 1:1 to 2:1.

Go beyond that and you're basically doomed—if you lose, say, 75% of your account then you need to quadruple your remaining cash just to get back to break-even. This can take years even with a sound trading method that makes a good risk-adjusted return, so it's essential that you do the following:

Stay as close to the left side of this chart as possible.

If you're going to put on 20 positions maximum, and risk 2% per position, then it means you are capping your maximum theoretical loss at about 40% of your account. For this to happen, all 20 of your positions would have to be exited as losers simultaneously. If you have included some inverse funds in your portfolio, then the chances of every single position being a loser simultaneously are very small. You are "hedged" against suffering your maximum loss.

Note that even this worse-case scenario of a 40% loss is still better than the maximum drawdown you would have encountered over the last ten years if you have been using a "buy and hold with no risk management" strategy.

In my experience with this kind of trading method, risking 2% per trade with a maximum of 20 positions is enough risk to have a chance of a reasonable return (say 15%), but also keeps drawdowns to a level that most people can tolerate and trade through (say 25%).

If you can tolerate bigger drawdowns and want a chance at bigger returns, then you can increase the risk per trade to 3%. If a 25% drawdown sounds like too much to you, then you should reduce the risk per trade to 1%, but understand that you are reducing your chances of making a 15% CAGR.

Exit Strategy

Once you are in a position, the only thing you have to worry about is when to get out. For buy-and-hold, the answer is never. For those who do the annual rebalancing ritual, the answer is "a bit every year, but only if it's gone up."

With a trend-capturing method, the time to get out is when it's likely that the trend you were trying to capture has ended, and has possibly reversed. The simplest way to determine this is with a trailing stop. Here's the rule:

$$10 * ATR(50) \text{ Trailing Stop Hit}$$

The initial stop on your position was calculated in the "Position Sizing" section as a ten times the ATR(50) stop. This is the maximum risk you will ever take on the position, and if price ever goes down to this point, you will exit. But what about a position that moves in your favor? How do you ensure you capture some of that profit before the market tumbles?

The answer is with a trailing stop. Rather than the exit price staying the same, as the price of the ETF goes up, so does the stop price—but it "trails" behind it. In the example SPY position earlier we calculated that we were taking $15.20 risk per share. This means that our initial stop would be our entry price minus $15.20. Therefore, if the entry price were $132.39, then the formula for the initial stop (exit price) would be

$$\text{Initial Stop Price} = \text{Entry Price} - \text{Initial Risk per Share}$$

$$\text{Initial Stop Price} = \$132.39 - \$15.20 = \$117.19$$

If the price of SPY closed below $117.19, you would exit the position the next day and take the loss. If the SPY closing price is higher than your entry price, then you would recalculate the stop as follows:

$$\text{Trailing Stop Price} = \text{Closing Price} - \text{Current Risk per Share}$$

$$\text{Current Risk per Share} = 10 * \text{Current ATR(50)}$$

Therefore, if the closing price were, say, $140, and the current ATR(50) were now 1.60, then the stop price would be calculated as follows:

$$\text{Trailing Stop Price} = \$140 - (10 * \$1.60) = \$124$$

This would mean you would move up your stop (exit) price to $124 and exit if SPY closed below this value. Whether you actually enter the stop prices into your brokerage account and allow them to be triggered intraday by your broker's trading platform is up to you. If you think you will forget to check your stops on all your positions periodically, then it's a good idea to put stops in with your broker. If you put all this into a spreadsheet and simply run it once a week to check your stops, then you can probably implement your exits manually without any issues.

A good compromise would be to put your initial stop into your brokerage account (as a good-until-cancelled [GTC] stop), but then manage your trailing stops on a spreadsheet and exit if any of them are hit. In this way you are making sure it is unlikely that you will suffer more than your maximum loss on any trade, but you don't have to keep adjusting lots of stops in your brokerage account.

Note that in all cases getting out close to your stop price is not guaranteed, but on average, your losing trades should be less than your maximum loss, because if they move in your favor at all after you get into the position, your stop will have trailed up from where it started. If you're concerned about not being able to get out close to your stop price, just think back to the situation you were in when you had no stops at all, were taking 100% risk on each position, and probably had your account fully invested all the time!

The occasional exit-beyond-your-stop price is insignificant compared to the way you were investing before.

That's it! The only exit strategy you really need. An ATR-based trailing stop will adapt to changes in volatility, move up to protect profits and reduce risk, and should never widen to go beyond your initial risk.

If you use XLQ and Excel to get historical price information for each of the ETFs in your portfolio, it's relatively simple to plot a chart with your trailing stop right on it so you can see when you should exit. An example of this is shown in Figure 5-6.

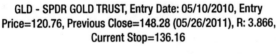

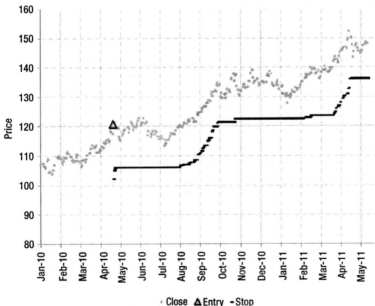

Figure 5-6. Example GLD position with trailing stop

Mr. and Mrs. Fit Become Part-Time Portfolio Managers

Mr. and Mrs. Fit decide to take control of their own investment performance and portfolio management. Mr. Fit now realizes that simply setting an allocation percentage in his retirement account and passively rebalancing each year provides very poor performance and takes large risks with his retirement cash. He also knows that paying a financial company an annual fee for implementing a similar procedure for him makes no sense—he'll still make a poor return but also be out the fee.

Mr. Fit makes a decision to find the time to actively manage his own investment accounts and puts a plan in place to acquire the required skills that he currently lacks in order to do this effectively. Mr. Fit has a personal computer and a spreadsheet program, but he is nowhere near an expert user, so he takes some online courses to significantly improve his spreadsheet formula skills. His aim is to become an "expert" user like Mrs. Fit.

Once he is much more competent at spreadsheet formulas, Mr. Fit downloads the free trial of XLQ so he can easily get historical price data into his spreadsheet. He spends a few weeks learning about all the new formulas he has access to via XLQ and builds some charts and tables that give him lots of information about various financial instruments.

Next, Mr. Fit uses a financial web site that has ETF information to construct his initial portfolio of tradable ETFs. He plugs each one into his spreadsheet and writes formulas that calculate the capital efficiency, the ten-day price move, and the ten-day ATR. He can use this information to signal when he should consider entering a new position. He looks at the list each evening to see how often he gets a new entry signal.

While he is waiting for his first entry signal, Mr. Fit programs the position-sizing calculation into his sheet. He inputs his account value and his risk per trade, and the spreadsheet formulas he wrote calculates how many shares he would buy and sell. He ranks the ETFs in the sheet in descending order by capital efficiency using the spreadsheet sort function so that he can take signals in ETFs that use up the least amount of capital first.

When Mr. Fit gets a signal to enter a position, the sheet tells him exactly how many shares to buy. He enters the order into his brokerage account and then puts the fill price into his sheet so he can calculate profit and loss for this position and track where his stop should be. He has already programmed a chart on his sheet that tracks the trailing stop, so he knows exactly where he will exit the trade before he even puts the position on. Since he is unable to monitor his account on a daily basis, Mr. Fit enters a GTC sell market order into his brokerage account so the position will be exited if it drops to his initial stop price (as calculated by the sheet).

Each weekend Mr. Fit updates his spreadsheet, checks for new entry signals, and recalculates his stops. If the stop price has changed for any of his existing positions, he amends the price on his GTC order. If any of his positions have been stopped out, he records that on his sheet so that he knows he can take another entry signal in that particular ETF now that he no longer has a position in it. Mr. Fit typically changes the color of the sheet tab to indicate whether he has a position in each of the ETFs in his portfolio. Mr. Fit has shown everything he has done to Mrs. Fit so she could manage their account properly if he was unable to do it for a period of time. Mrs. Fit also has the broker account password and understands how to manage stops and put on positions in the online access to the brokerage account.

As Mr. Fit gets more competent at writing spreadsheet formulas, he enhances his sheet to include lots of useful statistics about his account performance. He calculates the CAGR, the maximum drawdown, and exactly how much profit or loss each position is making right now. He has also designed a sheet that shows similar statistics for his "old" method of periodic rebalancing so he can compare how his account is performing, on a risk-adjusted basis of course, with the "old" way of doing things. None of this information is included on the standard account statement he receives, or in his online access to the account, so if he did not know how to do the calculations himself, he would have no real idea how well his account was performing on a risk-adjusted basis.

Mr. Fit is interested in finance now anyway, and he finds that he enjoys looking at his spreadsheet almost daily even though it only really requires 30 minutes of his time every weekend to manage his accounts. He decides that in the future he will implement a version of this method in a regular brokerage account where he has access to many more financial instruments and order types. Mr. Fit starts to learn about different instrument types like equities, bonds, and options.

Although in the short-term his investment results can be volatile, Mr. Fit sees that, over a reasonable period of time—say, five years—the MAR ratio of his active management trend-capturing method is significantly better than the FARCE method he was doing before. Mr. and Mrs. Fit laugh to themselves and can't believe that they had used such an inferior method for so long, and wonder why it took them so long to switch to something that actually had a good chance of success. The Fits know that success is not guaranteed with the method they use now, but they are confident that their chances of success are significantly improved as long as they accurately and consistently implement the method.

In Summary

In this chapter I've warned you that managing your own investment accounts is probably not a good idea for most people, but if you're going to do it anyway, then use the simplified trend-capturing approach I outline to maximize the chances of a reasonable risk-adjusted return compared to FARCE.

If you don't have the time or inclination to do this yourself consistently, then contact me for a referral to someone who can and will manage your money for a reasonable fee using similar (but more sophisticated) methods to those outlined here.

As mentioned, a complete trading approach has all six of the following components defined in detail:

- Market selection
- Instrument filter
- Setup conditions
- Entry signal
- Position sizing
- Exit strategy

If your approach does not include specific rules for all six components, then your results will be random (at best) and have a significantly negative expectation (at worst). Don't be one of the 95% of the poker players sending all their chips across the table to the professionals while the casino is taking their cut on every hand.

The bottom line is that it's well worth a 2% annual fee to put your money with a competent financial advisor as long as they are not using a traditional rebalancing approach. Unfortunately I only know of one financial advisor in the United States who is actually offering this kind of managed account solution for an annual asset management fee.

Taking Control

Procrastination Is a Leading Cause of Failure, So Take Action Now

If you've been implementing each step as you read this book, then all I can say is, "Well done. I'm impressed, and you don't need to read this chapter." If you're like most people, who find it hard to take action, even if they know it's important, then this chapter is just for you. I'm going to give you a complete summary of the actions you need to take to implement all the ideas in this book. I'll also list what I've presented so far in a simple and concise way so that you can act on it right now (assuming you have read and understood the rest of the book, of course).

Achieve Financial Fitness

Before you can even contemplate implementing any ideas to protect wealth, you have to generate some wealth in the first place. Nothing in this book can help you if you have a negative net worth, spend more than you earn each month, and don't have any savings. (That loose change you found down the back of the sofa doesn't count, by the way.)

There are two main aspects to financial fitness:

1. Positive monthly cash flow

2. Positive net worth

Number 1 is achieved by having monthly income greater than monthly expenses. If you spend more than you earn, there are only two ways to make this simple math add up:

Spend less or earn more.

It's that simple. Once you accept that all spending decisions are under your direct control, it's just a matter of changing your current choices so that your total expense number adds up to less than your current income. Note that this may mean that you cannot currently afford some of the products or services you've been used to in the past, but this is just math—the numbers don't lie. Once you've reached equilibrium (i.e., your monthly expenses are equal to your monthly income) then don't stop—keep at it so that you can generate a surplus of cash on a monthly basis. You can then put that surplus straight into a savings account and start accumulating some wealth that needs to be protected.

Once you've achieved number 1 and you're saving on a monthly basis, then number 2 will take care of itself—it's only a matter of time. Eventually the savings you accumulate will end up being greater than any current liabilities you have, and you will eventually achieve a positive net worth. At this point you have reached financial fitness and can move on to more interesting parts of the action plan—how to effectively protect the wealth you have created.

Create an Emergency Fund

Once you're cash flow positive, you're saving each month, and you have a positive net worth, it's important to have some funds set aside for emergencies. This means that if you lose your job, incur some significant uninsured medical expenses, have any kind of financial emergency, or simply want to have peace of mind about your financial situation, then you need a place to keep that emergency cash where it won't simply get eaten away by inflation coupled with a low rate of return. The idea is to make sure it's still worth something when you need it.

This is step 1 of the action plan, presented in Chapter 3, and simply tells you not to leave your emergency fund in cash in a checking or savings account earning a negative real rate of return. If you can't remember what this means, please read Chapter 3 again in detail.

For people with equity in a home they own, putting a HELOC in place is a good solution. The important thing to remember if you choose to implement this version of the plan is to do it *before* an emergency occurs. Like any property-based loan, a HELOC is a loan against your current income that is secured by a property (so you get a better rate of interest). If you have no income, then you can't get a loan, period. Going to the bank and asking for a HELOC after you lose your job is simply a waste of time. Your emergency fund could consist of the (unused as yet) line of credit and an investment in precious metals (see the following list).

If you don't have any home equity, then your emergency fund should be implemented by funding a GoldMoney account and putting the cash equally into the four metals it currently supports:

- Gold
- Silver
- Palladium
- Platinum

Each time you add to the account you should buy an equal dollar value of each metal with the contribution. Although the value of this type of portfolio will be volatile in the short term, it has a much better chance of maintaining purchasing power in the long term. This is the main objective of your emergency fund.

You should initially contribute cash that represents at least 6 months worth of expenses, but 12 months would be a better target. Remember to adjust the fund if your monthly expenses increase significantly for any reason.

Fund a Savings Account

Once you have your emergency fund in place, any surplus cash really becomes true savings that you can start to put to use, or allocate to future major spending requirements. This was step 2, for which Chapter 4 outlined an effective method to manage a savings account. For this cash, the main objective is not simply to maintain purchasing power (as with your emergency fund), but to generate a positive real rate of return with minimal volatility (i.e., risk).

The way to do this is to alternate between the following two financial instrument classes:

- Major international currencies
- Precious metals ETFs

The method switches between the two instrument types depending on prevailing interest rates and inflation rates (represented by the CPI relevant to each country or geographic region's currency).

The ten currencies used are:

- Australian dollar
- British pound
- Canadian dollar
- Euro
- Hong Kong dollar
- Japanese yen
- New Zealand dollar
- Swedish krona
- Swiss franc
- United States dollar

The six ETFs used are:

- Gold (GLD)
- Silver (SLV)
- Platinum (PPLT)
- Palladium (PALL)
- Inverse Treasury Bonds (TBT)
- Treasury Inflation Protected Securities (TIP)

The rule for switching between the two is as follows:

If at least eight out of the ten currencies are paying interest at least 2% above the rate of inflation in that country or region, then you should invest in currencies. Otherwise invest in the ETFs.

Using this method should give you a good chance of realizing a decent real rate of return and should minimize volatility at the same time. This is a good compromise between taking zero risk (by simply keeping the cash in dollars) and taking 100% risk by using buy-and-hold investing, or some sort of periodic rebalancing of a diversified portfolio of assets. Note that just keeping your savings in cash (or cash equivalents like certificates of deposit) will generate a negative real rate of return if inflation is greater than the interest payable, so it's not really zero risk—it's a guaranteed loss of purchasing power.

Remember that risk and reward go hand in hand, and there is no such thing as a free lunch—any method involves the risk of losing value in order to generate some kind of return. The main question you need to address is whether you are receiving a reasonable real return for the risk you are taking.

Manage Your Investment Accounts

Once you have a surplus of savings and there are no further spending requirements to be saved for, then additional cash may be allocated to investment accounts. This also includes any contributions to a retirement account you may have already made, or have been making while implementing the rest of the items in this action plan.

A key point made in step 3 in Chapter 5, on investment management, is that traditional approaches like dollar cost averaging, buy-and-hold, and FARCE have very poor risk-adjusted return and should be avoided. In fact, if your employer is making matching contributions to your retirement account, for example, then it's fine to simply treat that as your return on investment and put your entire account into the money market fund.

If you do want to actively manage your investment accounts, then it's essential that you have a complete and sophisticated approach that includes all the major components of a trading program. These are:

- Market selection
- Instrument filter
- Setup conditions
- Entry signal
- Position sizing
- Exit strategy

Chapter 5 explained each of these components in detail and outlined a complete method for effectively managing an investment account. The best way to implement the investment management strategy is in a spreadsheet program using XLQ to get data automatically. If you don't have the required financial or spreadsheet skills to do this on your own, then you can either learn them or contact me for a referral to someone who can manage your account for you for a fee.

The important thing to remember is that simplistic or traditional portfolio management methods don't work well, and you're better off not having any investment accounts at all, and just stopping at step 2 of the plan if you don't have the skills (or don't want to learn the skills) to implement the method presented in Chapter 5.

If you follow the method presented in Chapter 5 consistently and accurately, then you should have a much better chance of a decent risk-adjusted return than any other method you can easily implement in your account on your own. No method can guarantee success, and any method that attempts to control risk will significantly underperform one that takes 100% risk at times, especially if we're in a raging bull market and everything is going up.

But what I can guarantee is that the next time the S&P 500 index goes down 60% (or more), any accounts using the method presented in this book will perform considerably better (on a risk-adjusted-return basis) than buy-and-hold or FARCE strategies.

What Could Go Wrong?

All the methods and ideas presented in this book are designed to adapt to changes in market conditions, interest rates, inflation rates, and market volatility. This means that as long as the rules of the game don't significantly change, you should not have to adapt or modify what you are doing. However, it's possible that future government, business, and banking decisions or events will mean that some of the methods in this book are no longer viable. In this section I will discuss some of the possible problems and outline simple solutions.

The first list of items are things that have happened in the past or could happen in the future. But they do not mean it's a financial Armageddon and we're now in a barter economy where your domestic currency is gone forever.

It's No Longer Legal for Citizens of Your Country to Own Precious Metals

If your government changes the rules to prevent its citizens from owning physical precious metals, then you need to either go live in another country, or switch your emergency fund into your savings account and use metals ETFs instead of the physical metal.

GoldMoney Or Your Metals Broker Goes Out of Business

It's a fact of life that there is no free lunch—every financial decision has some risk involved. If GoldMoney does go out of business and with it your emergency fund, it does not mean the method of owning precious metals is invalid. It just means that we chose a poor implementation. My advice would be to build up another emergency fund (or use your savings to replenish your emergency fund) and find an alternative way of owning physical precious metals.

Some of the Major Currencies Become Defunct

Throughout history, currencies have been born and then died. There is no reason why some of the currencies currently being used for your savings might not become defunct. It's unlikely, but possible. If this happens, then either simply drop that currency from the list, or replace it with the new currency that has been created to replace the old one. People in that country will still need a currency. And don't get too depressed—compare this situation to the one you would be in if you had all your savings in a currency that became defunct, rather than just a relatively small proportion.

Some of the Precious Metals ETFs No Longer Exist or Have Very Low Volume

If some of the precious metals or bond ETFs being used in the savings method end up having very low volume or become defunct, then it will probably mean that the volume has shifted somewhere else. Either drop that ETF from the list (if there is no new alternative ETF) or switch to similar ETFs where all the liquidity has migrated.

Some of the ETFs in Your Investment Portfolio No Longer Exist or Have Very Low Volume

The solution to low or zero volume in some of the ETFs in your investment portfolio is the same as for the savings ETFs—exit any open positions and then reevaluate the list of ETFs in your portfolio to find where the liquidity has migrated to. If you perform this task on a periodic basis anyway, your portfolio will already be adapting to where the volume currently is.

Your Broker Goes Out of Business

Again, it's a fact that brokers do go out of business. If this happens, it doesn't invalidate your investment method. Chalk it up to experience, take whatever assets you're left with, and try again with another broker.

If something significant does change in the future that invalidates some of the methods contained in this book in ways I have not covered here, then I'll plan to write and publish a new edition that addresses them. Until that happens, feel free to contact me for my ideas on how I have personally adapted to changes that have occurred. My contact details can be found on my web site, at http://pmkingtrading.com.

I'll also be providing any relevant updates on my trading, finance, and money-related blog, at www.pmkingtrading.com/wordpress.

Financial Meltdown

There are some who view the economic scene these days with increasing alarm, and speak and write in apocalyptic terms. I wouldn't lose sleep over this. But if there is a total financial meltdown—if your currency is totally mismanaged by your government and you end up with hyperinflation followed by a worthless currency—then there is not much you can do other than leave (if you can) and take any physical assets you still own with you if possible.

Plan to return if and when "normal" operation of your country's financial system resumes. If this is a global monetary system meltdown, then I'm afraid I have little advice at all other than to convert any remaining assets you have into one of the four necessities of life:

- Water
- Food
- Shelter
- Clothing

If you do this, then you also need to put measures in place to protect those assets from anyone else who has not had the foresight to put a survival plan in place. This is not a book about how to plan to survive a financial Armageddon, so I'll leave it at that.

In Summary

This chapter was a concise wrap-up of everything you need to do to implement the ideas in this book. The main action items were:

- Achieve financial fitness
- Create an emergency fund
- Manage your savings effectively
- Manage your investments effectively
- Adapt to changes in rules or market liquidity

The key idea is that you must start now if you're ever going to implement this plan. None of the steps are particularly difficult, but if you don't start doing something, they will never get done. You are in control and only you can make these kinds of decisions about your own financial future. Take action now.

I wish you success with your finances and investing, and I sincerely hope this book has been useful to you.

Recommended Reading

I have read quite a few investing- and trading-related books over the years (probably over 200 by now), and this Appendix contains the ones I recommend because they have something really useful to say.

Trading

21 Irrefutable Truths of Trading: A Trader's Guide to Developing a Mind to Win, The, by John Hayden (McGraw-Hill, 2000).

A Random Walk Down Wall Street: The Time-Tested Strategy for Successful Investing, by Burton Malkiel (W. W. Norton & Company, 2011).

Beyond Candlesticks: New Japanese Charting Techniques Revealed, by Steve Nison (Wiley, 1994).

Campaign Trading: Tactics and Strategies to Exploit the Markets, by John Sweeney (Wiley, 1996).

Complete Guide to Building a Successful Trading Business, The, by Paul M. King (PMKing Trading LLC, 2007).

Recommended Reading

Complete TurtleTrader: How 23 Novice Investors Became Overnight Millionaires, The, by Michael W. Covel (Harper Paperbacks, 2009).

DayTrading into the Millennium, by Michael Turner (M.P. Turner, 1998).

Education of a Speculator, The, by Victor Niederhoffer (Wiley, 1998).

Electronic Day Trader: Successful Strategies for On-line Trading, The, by Marc Friedfertig and George West (McGraw-Hill, 2000).

Electronic Day Trading to Win, by Bob Baird and Craig McBurney (Wiley, 1999).

Encyclopedia of Trading Strategies, The, by Jeffrey Owen Katz and Donna L. McCormick (McGraw-Hill, 2000).

Financial Freedom Through Electronic Day Trading, by Van K. Tharp and Brian June (McGraw-Hill, 2000).

Fooled by Randomness: The Hidden Role of Chance in Life and in the Markets, by Nassim Nicholas Taleb (Random House, 2008).

Fortune's Formula: The Untold Story of the Scientific Betting System That Beat the Casinos and Wall Street, by William Poundstone (Hill and Wang, 2006).

Hedgehogging, by Barton Biggs (Wiley, 2008).

How I Trade for a Living, by Gary Smith (Wiley, 1999).

Intermarket Analysis: Profiting from Global Market Relationships, by John Murphy (Wiley, 2004).

Irrational Exuberance, by Robert Shiller (Crown Business, 2006).

Japanese Candlestick Charting Techniques, Second Edition, by Steve Nison (Prentice Hall, 2001).

Liar's Poker, by Michael Lewis (W. W. Norton & Company, 2010).

Market Wizards: Interviews with Top Traders, by Jack D. Schwager (Marketplace Books, 2006).

Mastering the Trade: Proven Techniques for Profiting from Intraday and Swing Trading Setups, by John Carter (McGraw-Hill, 2005).

Mindtraps: Unlocking the Key to Investment Success, by Roland Barach (International Institute of Trading Mastery, 2000).

(Mis)behavior of Markets: A Fractal View of Risk, Ruin, and Reward, The, by Benoit Manelbrot and Richard L. Hudson (Basic Books, 2004).

New Market Wizards: Conversations with America's Top Traders, The, by Jack D. Schwager (Marketplace Books, 2008).

New Thinking in Technical Analysis: Trading Models from the Masters, by Rick Bensignor (editor) (Bloomberg Press, 2000).

Practical Speculation, by Victor Niederhoffer and Laurel Kenner (Wiley, 2005).

Psychology of Trading: Tools and Techniques for Minding the Markets, The, by Brett N. Steenbarger (Wiley, 2002).

Reminiscences of a Stock Operator, by Edwin Lefèvre and Roger Lowenstein (Wiley, 2006).

Rules of the Trade: Indispensable Insights for Online Profits, by David S. Nassar (McGraw-Hill, 2001).

Running Money: Hedge Fund Honchos, Monster Markets and My Hunt for the Big Score, by Andy Kessler (HarperCollins, 2004).

Schwager on Futures: Fundamental Analysis, by Steven C. Turner and Jack D. Schwager (Wiley, 1996).

Schwager on Futures: Technical Analysis, by Jack D. Schwager (Wiley, 1997).

Smarter Trading: Improving Performance in Changing Markets, by Perry Kaufman (McGraw-Hill, 1995).

Stock Market Wizards: Interviews with America's Top Stock Traders, by Jack D. Schwager (Marketplace Books, 2008).

Strategic Electronic Day Trader, The, by Robert Deel (Wiley, 2000).

Trade Your Way to Financial Freedom, by Van K. Tharp (McGraw-Hill, 2006).

Trader Vic: Methods of a Wall Street Master, by Victor Sperandeo (Wiley, 1993).

Trading in the Zone: Master the Market with Confidence, Discipline and a Winning Attitude, by Mark Douglas (Prentice Hall, 2001).

Trading Systems That Work: Building and Evaluating Effective Trading Systems, by Thomas Stridsman (McGraw-Hill, 2000).

Trend Following: Learn to Make Millions in Up or Down Markets, by Michael W. Covel (FT Press, 2009).

Way of the Turtle: The Secret Methods that Turned Ordinary People into Legendary Traders, The, by Curtis Faith (McGraw-Hill, 2007).

What Works in Online Trading, by Mark Etzkorn (Wiley, 2001).

When Genius Failed: The Rise and Fall of Long-Term Capital Management, by Roger Lowenstein (Random House Trade Paperbacks, 2001).

Money and Investing

Contrarian Investing: Buy and Sell When Others Won't and Make Money Doing It, by Anthony Gallea and William Patalon III (Prentice Hall, 1999).

Fiat Paper Money, by Ralph T. Foster (Ralph T. Foster, 2008).

Guerrilla Investing: Winning Strategies for Beating the Wall Street Professionals, by Peter Siris (Taylor Trade Publishing, 2000).

Investing for Dummies, Fifth Edition, by Eric Tyson (Wiley, 2008).

Investment Gurus: A Road Map to Wealth from the World's Best Money Managers, by Peter J. Tanous (Prentice Hall, 1999).

Money Game, The, by Adam Smith (Vintage, 1976).

Money Masters, The, by John Train (HarperBusiness, 1994).

New Rules of Money: 88 Simple Strategies for Financial Success Today, The, by Ric Edelman (Collins, 1999).

Pied Pipers of Wall Street: How Analysts Sell You Down the River, The, by Benjamin Mark Cole (Bloomberg Press, 2001).

Safe Strategies for Financial Freedom, by Van K. Tharp, D. R. Barton, Jr., and Steve Sjuggerud (McGraw-Hill, 2004).

Miscellaneous

Art of War, The, by Sun Tzu (translated by Samuel Griffith) (Oxford University Press, 1963).

Black Swan: The Impact of the Highly Improbable, The, by Nassim Nicholas Taleb (Random House, 2007).

Blink: The Power of Thinking Without Thinking, by Malcolm Gladwell (Back Bay Books, 2007).

Labyrinths of Reason: Paradox, Puzzles and the Frailty of Knowledge, by William Poundstone (Anchor, 1989).

Probability Without Tears: A Primer for Non-Mathematicians, by Derek Rowntree (Prentice Hall, 1984).

Way of The Warrior-Trader: The Financial Risk-Taker's Guide to Samurai Courage, Confidence and Discipline, The, by Richard D. McCall (McGraw-Hill, 1997).

Why Café, The, by John Strelecky (Aspen Light Publishing, 2011).

Useful Resources

While this list of resources may look a bit sparse, I've cut it down to only the really useful resources I use all the time, rather than including a huge list of everything to do with money and investing online.

Trading and Investments

pmkingtrading.com

finance.yahoo.com

Precious Metals

www.goldmoney.com

globalgold.ch

www.perthmint.com.au

bullionvault.com

Brokers

interactivebrokers.com

Economics and Statistics

www.shadowstats.com

www.tradingeconomics.com

www.economist.com

Currency Interest Rates and Consumer Price Indexes

AUD: www.abs.gov.au

CAD: www.statcan.gc.ca

CHF: www.bfs.admin.ch

EUR: epp.eurostat.ec.europa.eu

GBP: www.statistics.gov.uk

HKD: www.censtatd.gov.hk

JPY: www.e-stat.go.jp

NZD: www.rbnz.govt.nz

SEK: www.scb.se

USD: www.bls.gov

Products

qmatix.com

tradingblox.com

office.microsoft.com

I

Index

CPSIA information can be obtained at www.ICGtesting.com
Printed in the USA
LVOW060136091111

254149LV00001B/64/P